EARLY CHILDHOOD EDUCATION SERIES

Sharon Ryan, *Editor*

To look for other titles in this series, visit www.tcpress.com

(continued)

CONTINUITY IN CHILDREN'S WORLDS

CHOICES AND CONSEQUENCES FOR EARLY CHILDHOOD SETTINGS

MELISSA M. JOZWIAK
BETSY J. CAHILL
RACHEL THEILHEIMER

Foreword by Beth Blue Swadener

TEACHERS COLLEGE PRESS

TEACHERS COLLEGE | COLUMBIA UNIVERSITY
NEW YORK AND LONDON

Published by Teachers College Press, 1234 Amsterdam Avenue, New York, NY 10027

Cover design by Holly Grundon / BHG Graphic Design. Photo by FamVeld from Thinkstock by Getty Images.

Library of Congress Cataloging-in-Publication Data is available at loc.gov

Names: Jozwiak, Melissa M., 1971- author. I Cahill, Betsy J., author. I
    Theilheimer, Rachel, author.
Title: Continuity in children's worlds : choices and consequences for early
    childhood settings / Melissa M. Jozwiak, Betsy J. Cahill, Rachel Theilheimer.
Description: New York, NY : Teachers College Press, 2016. I Series: Early
    childhood education series I Includes bibliographical references and index.
Identifiers: LCCN 2016003200 (print) I LCCN 2016015715 (ebook) I ISBN
    9780807757895 (pbk. : alk. paper) I ISBN 9780807774939 (ebook)
Subjects: LCSH: Early childhood education. I Readiness for school. I Child
    psychology. I Child development.
Classification: LCC LB1139.23 .J69 2016 (print) I LCC LB1139.23 (ebook) I DDC
    372.21—dc23
LC record available at https://lccn.loc.gov/2016003200

ISBN 978-0-8077-5789-5 (paper)
ISBN 978-0-8077-7493-9 (ebook)

Printed on acid-free paper
Manufactured in the United States of America

23 22 21 20 19 18 17 16   8 7 6 5 4 3 2 1

Contents

Foreword

Continuity in Children's Worlds is a book about relationships and the emotional lives of children, families, and caregivers, constructed around stories that are compelling in their familiarity and the sensitivity with which they are written and unpacked. Building on longtime collaborative relationships and experiences in child care settings in several states, the authors complicate rather than simplify or reify continuity of care, staffing, programs, and home–school life worlds of children through stories and counter stories. Through accessible writing and nuanced discussion of stories, this volume engages readers in a series of queries that often raise more questions than they answer, and in doing so it complicates the literature on continuity of care in important ways. A major strength of the book is the authors' resistance to the explicit guidelines and pervasive binaries in the field as reflected in debates over "best practice," including what constitutes developmentally appropriate practice and what represents quality (e.g., Cannella, Perez, & Lee, 2016; Dahlberg, Moss, & Pence, 1999; Nagasawa, Peters, & Swadener, 2014). *Continuity in Children's Worlds* is also about cultures and the nuanced dynamics of home–school continuities and discontinuities, as well as the diversities among staff in child care settings, as they relate to views, policies, and practices that shape continuity of care in local contexts.

My recent collaboration in a 3-year study of relationships-based caregiving in infant and toddler centers, drawing from the work of Lally (2013) and others, was designed, in part, to promote a child rights–based framework and emphasize continuity of caregiving, small groups, children's ability to interact with one another, and changes in the environment to promote less containment and more engagement with activities and interactions between children. In many cases, this meant directors and teachers grappling with pervasive practices that tend to emphasize efficiency in staffing, budgetary constraints, or assumptions of infant and toddler-being that ran counter to the project's goals. As participants became more informed about child-focused practices, most worked to institute practices including primary caregiving, schedule and environmental changes, and better communication with families with a focus on the well-being of children (Peters, Gaches, & Swadener, 2015). As I read this book, I wished that the current volume had been available to share with participating child care teachers and directors and our project team.

The power of story and of counter stories is evident in the pages to follow. Drawn from the coauthors' experiences across time and settings and their discussion of their attempts to enact continuity of care, this volume offers practical insights for community-based work in center-based and kith-and-kin-care settings, teacher education, and early childhood research. While continuity-of-care practices do not guarantee strong relationships among caregivers, children, and families, as the authors observe, the promise of attention to continuities and discontinuities in care and across home and child care settings offers insights into everyday situations, challenges, and successes that strengthen programs as well as relationships. The implicit and explicit critique of pervasive binaries was also an important reminder to readers that prescriptive checklists and guidelines for continuity often tell only a small part of the story. The authors' case for decentering assumptions and increasing comfort with discontinuity was also refreshing and honest.

Books that convey respect for children as full human beings whose emotions, experiences, and perspectives must be given due weight are critical in these neoliberal times when earlier reading, more assessment, and increasingly narrow "readiness" discourses and policies (Iorio & Parnell, 2015) have become master scripts in our field. While this book offers no quick fixes or formulas, it does offer hope through its rich and abundant examples of teachers, parents, and others who care for young children mindfully taking the time to address issues of continuity in everyday life. Many of us will find ourselves, our commitments, and our dilemmas as caregivers, teachers, allies, advocates, and childhood studies researchers in this volume—I know that I did.

—Beth Blue Swadener

REFERENCES

Cannella, G. S., Perez, M. S., & Lee, I. (2016). *Critical examinations of quality in early education and care: Regulation, disqualification, and erasure.* New York, NY: Peter Lang.

Dahlberg, G., Moss, P., & Pence, A. (1999). *Beyond quality in early childhood education and care: Languages of evaluation.* New York, NY: Routledge.

Iorio, J. M., & Parnell, W. (2015). *Rethinking readiness in early childhood education: Implications for policy and practice.* New York, NY: Palgrave Macmillan.

Nagasawa, M., Peters, L., & Swadener, B. B. (2014). The costs of putting quality first: Neoliberalism, (in)equality, (un)affordability, and (in)accessibility? In

M. Bloch, B. B. Swadener, & G. Cannella (Eds.), *Reconceptualizing early childhood care and education: Critical questions, new imaginaries and social activism* (pp. 277–288). New York, NY: Peter Lang,

Peters, L., Gaches, S., & Swadener, B. B. (2015). Narratives on children's rights and well-being. *He Kupa Early Childhood eJournal, 4*(2), 58–70.

Acknowledgments

Marie Ellen Larcada gave us initial support when this book was merely an idea. Sarah Biondello nurtured us and this project along the way. John Bylander helped us to see it to completion.

The teachers and faculty with whom we had our first continuity conversation sent our minds whirling in several directions and compelled us to think deeply about continuity and discontinuity. We are grateful to them for that. Over the course of our writing, college students, colleagues, and friends gave us feedback on some of the stories in this book, providing us additional insights.

We are appreciative of conference participants who generously shared their stories of continuity and discontinuity. Alayne Stieglitz, Virginia Casper, Helen Frazier, and Liege Motta expressed enthusiasm for our project and led us to storytellers whom we would not have encountered otherwise. Alayne assisted in innumerable ways, most important, providing invaluable feedback on Chapter 2.

Our families supported us throughout this project as we collected data, analyzed them, and wrote together over the vast geographic distance and different time zones. They lived with our long phone calls and our periodic meetings in various locations across the country. Thank you and love to Andy, Nicholas, and Lauren, to Eve and Jesse, and to Jonathan.

And finally our deepest thanks to the many educators and parents who told us about their lives with children and the ways in which continuity and discontinuity have figured in them.

CONTINUITY IN CHILDREN'S WORLDS

CHAPTER 1

Introduction
Continuity, Consistency, and the Need for Flexibility

When you were young, you probably enjoyed having someone tell you a story or read you a book. As you listened, you may have imagined yourself as a wild thing roaring your terrible roar and gnashing your terrible teeth, as in *Where the Wild Things Are* (Sendak, 1963), or as a child poking snow down from a tree with a stick, as in *The Snowy Day* (Keats, 1976). As an adult, it may not be as easy to picture yourself in the story; however, we hope that, as you read this book, you will do just that. This is a book of stories. The stories it tells will help you ponder the many ways in which questions of continuity and discontinuity arise in children's worlds and in the lives of the people who care for and educate them.

Over the course of several years, early childhood professionals and parents from across the country told us stories about their experience with continuity and discontinuity. Their stories have helped us investigate beliefs about continuity and discontinuity and how they are enacted in contexts for children from birth to age 8. The stories and what we, the authors, write about them reveal a range of continuities and discontinuities, including the experiences children, teachers, administrators, and families have at programs. The stories define continuity and discontinuity in a variety of ways—for example, as sameness and difference and as comfort and challenge. We look at the interactions between families and schools and among teachers, and the ways in which programs and schools relate to each other. Stories about continuity and discontinuity shed light on and raise questions about the work of early childhood educators on the individual, group, and systems levels. For example, stories describe children's transitions (home to school, classroom to classroom, school to school) and raise questions about primary caregiving, cultural responsiveness, assessment, and congruity between institutions. These stories make up only a small, fragmented view of the actual events. They are often a partial recounting that cannot tell us all we want to know about an event or answer all our questions.

Nonetheless, they provide insight into what the storyteller knows, believes, and experiences regarding continuity and discontinuity.

A BOOK OF STORIES

Each chapter presents continuity stories, sometimes from more than one perspective, to provoke thinking and inform decisionmaking. Although we continue to define and redefine continuity in the pages that follow, here we offer beginning definitions, ways to think about continuity and discontinuity, as we introduce the first stories. Continuity is a connection, a flow between two things. Discontinuity can be a break, separation, or lack of connection. The following story shows how one director thought about the two.

Nursery School

When I left the infant program, I took a new position at a school that follows a traditional nursery school model. I found that the young 2-year-olds there came only 2 mornings a week and the older 2s came 3 mornings. I think this scheduling system is nuts; however, the teachers do a heck of a job. They have a very long phase-in period, and the teachers help children with managing coming only 2 or 3 days. I plan to suggest changing the schedule next year, and I think teachers will be happy to get to know only one group of children who come all 5 mornings.

The director telling this story worries that the children who attend for only a few hours a day, every other day, lack the continuity that a 5-day schedule provides. The teachers try to increase continuity between home and school with a long phase-in period to transition children into the program. Yet the children who negotiate the changes between home and school two or three times a week—with gaps in between each day at school—may experience discontinuity. This director proposes changes to address the continuity-discontinuity dynamic and, in so doing, will create some discontinuity for the program and the teachers. Although their director thinks the teachers will ultimately appreciate the new scheduling, the teachers are used to the 2- and 3-day schedules. For them, a change will mean adjusting to a new rhythm and will create discontinuity. This story is just one example of the ways in which continuity and discontinuity are inextricable. Creating continuity here means creating discontinuity as well.

The next story illustrates what a parent found appealing in a program that has recently made a comparable scheduling change.

The Selling Point

After spending 5 years as a principal of a preschool, moving to Florida and finding a program for my 3-year-old son that suited both my needs and his was a new challenge. Up until this point, I had always known exactly where he would be and the teachers he would be with. . . . I had hired them.

Therefore, you would think a school that had been running for 25 years, staff members who had been there 10-plus years, and a program that had earned a strong reputation in the community would seem ideal for this ex-principal/ex-teacher, new-to-the-community, first-time mom. The funny thing was, none of that seemed to matter to me. What sold me on the program was what I learned when I was touring with the director. She was not new to being a director, but she was new to the position in this school and only going into her 2nd year.

For the first time since they had opened, decades ago, the Mother's Day Out program and the preschool program were operating independently from one another. The staff was undergoing schedule changes, new expectations in policies and procedures, and extensive training to a new preschool curriculum. If this does not scream discontinuity among an early childhood community, I don't know what does. Then I asked about staff turnover; the answer was "minimal." I asked about drop in enrollment. The answer was "The school is only growing."

For me, the idea of changes in program, routine, goals, and expectations reveals a community that desires to improve and be better. A school environment that does not value different points of view and open-mindedness is not a school I want my child to be a part of. The fact that this kind of evolution was being accomplished with little turnover in staff and a boost in enrollment confirmed for me that the direction of the school was placed in capable hands. So, in a way, the discontinuity in the school environment was actually the selling point.

This parent was drawn to a program because of the way it approached discontinuity. She regarded discontinuity as an openness to change, to reevaluation, and to ongoing improvement. Her story parallels our intentions in this book—to show the multiple ways continuity and discontinuity interact and how early childhood educators and the families of young children can value both continuity and discontinuity for different reasons.

These two stories highlight the types of conversations you will find throughout the book. Discussion of each story within the text illustrates the complexity of the issues and raises questions about the educator's role. Each chapter includes stories, our interpretations and connections to relevant literature, and questions for reflection and implications for practice.

Continuity

The early childhood literature often describes continuity as a desirable quality or characteristic (Child Care Aware of America, 2015; Institute of Medicine & National Research Council, 2015; Kagan, 1991; Kagan & Tarrant, 2010; Mayfield, 2003; National Association for the Education of Young Children, 2009). Many of the stories we heard express this view as well. In the pages that follow, you will read stories from individuals who want to see greater continuity across early childhood practices, curriculum, and settings. Others seek continuity between what they believe and their daily interactions with children. Expressed in different ways and in different contexts, at least some early educators and families told us they want connectedness and consistency. Their stories evoke such questions as, "Why do children need a predictable daily routine that results in a sense of continuity in the flow of their day?" and "How does knowing more about families' lives help a teacher do a better job with the children in her class?" Or, "What could I, as a kindergarten teacher, do with assessment data from preschool about the children in my class?" and "How does my experience in a teacher education program prepare me for the realities of the classroom?"

Discontinuity

When one views discontinuity as a rupture, a change in the flow, or chaos, one might assume that discontinuity and continuity are mutually exclusive and exist independently of each other. With the premise, then, that continuity is valuable, some early educators have written about solving the problem of discontinuity (e.g., Lombardi, 1992). In contrast, like the parent who told us the story "The Selling Point," we step back and wonder if discontinuity always needs to be remedied. For example, to what degree is it a problem for children to move between different settings, and why? And if it is a problem, is continuity the answer? Can we separate continuity from discontinuity? Our first story, "Nursery School," suggests that we cannot. And, if we respect difference and diversity, can we justifiably call for continuity that might lead instead to homogenization?

As you read this book, do not look for simple answers to these and other questions. Rather, use this book as a guided query in which we present continuity and discontinuity from different angles, through the voices of practitioners and parents, some of whom do not agree and some of whom contest or challenge current early childhood practices. The purpose of this book is to encourage a deeper understanding of the complexities inherent in work with young children, colleagues, and families. We hope that, as a result of reading it, our readers will feel better equipped to thoughtfully consider and critically reflect on the impact that continuity and discontinuity have on the early childhood years and on the adults who work with and care about young children. As you read, think about your stories of continuity and discontinuity. Where do they fit into the chapters that follow?

The Stories and Best Practice

At times, the parents' and teachers' stories connect with and support what researchers and scholars have written about continuity and best practice, as you will see in this next story.

The Broken Cracker

He started in the infant room when he was a year old. He had experienced homelessness, violence, and the effects of substance abuse. The team began working with him on his issues around food. For example, they knew that if he had a broken cracker, he would fall apart. When a teacher noticed that his cracker was broken, she would subtly replace it. It was a seamless movement of a caregiver's knowing what a child needed before it became a problem for him. The team artfully predicted his needs and met them. The children do not have to go to extremes to get their needs met when caregivers know the children.

Knowing a child well, as these teachers did, and responding accordingly is a fundamental goal of continuity of care, discussed in depth in the next chapter. Although treating one child differently from the rest may not sit well with all practitioners, these teachers believed that treating all children fairly does not mean treating them all the same. Most early childhood educators would agree that the groundwork for good practice depends upon getting to know individual children well and acting toward them based on that knowledge.

However, not all the stories practitioners and families told us match professional writing about early childhood, as the next story demonstrates.

Individual Circumstances

The diversity of our center means that "best practices" don't always work for us. We have to be flexible. When a child came in late and was hungry, staff invited the parent to join the child for something to eat instead of dispensing a lecture about the value of getting to school on time for breakfast. The teachers had to get over asking children and families to do all the changing and instead be open, adapting the program to the children and families. We bent our policies to the children and families' needs and everyone recognized that this is neither unfair nor spoiling the child. This has always been, and continues to be, something that is discussed frequently at the center: the contradiction between the need for continuity and consistency and the need for flexibility and consideration of individual circumstances.

Consistency and predictability can help a classroom run smoothly. Yet flexibility and adaptation to individual circumstances enables programs to fit children and families instead of the other way around.

The interplay of continuity and discontinuity inspired this book. In the next section, we share our story with you: how this work on continuity began, why it is important to us, and what we have learned. The last section shows how joining in this examination of continuity could affect you as an early childhood professional, helping you to understand the complexity associated with a concept that is frequently cited but rarely examined with the critical considerations it requires.

OUR STORY

When our story began, we never imagined that one conversation on a Friday afternoon would lead to so many new conversations about continuity and, ultimately, to this book.

Complicating What We Read

We met with teachers from the university laboratory school to talk about continuity, because, for several years, the program had been looping one toddler teacher to the preschool room with the children who were old enough to move to the next room. One preschool teacher would then move to the toddler classroom so each room had continuity between at least one teacher and the children in that classroom. As administrators, we wondered if this was the best thing to do for our children and our teachers because we had observed that some teachers did better with some age groups than with others. Also, we heard teachers express frustration with having to break up teaching teams that were working well to make room for the teacher who was looping with the children. No one expressed concern that this was a bad idea for the children, but we certainly were unsure when we considered it from the teacher's perspective.

The literature on toddler care supported the practice of looping, but our reality complicated what we had read. This realization inspired us to invite the teachers to join us for a conversation about continuity. We invited each teacher, administrator, and faculty member to share a continuity story from his or her work or personal life. To our surprise, it was a long meeting. No one seemed to want to stop talking about continuity and discontinuity.

As we reviewed the stories, we marveled at their breadth. Some of the stories reflected what we had read in the literature about continuity, for example, about continuity of care and transitions, and others generated new ways to think about continuity.

Complexity

The stories illustrated complexity—complexity that early childhood educators face daily. For example, as you saw earlier, continuity for the child can result in discontinuity for the teacher. The values that promote continuity or discontinuity lead to complexity as well. While continuity can lead children and families to trust early childhood educators, discontinuity promotes growth and learning. Discontinuity in the form of diversity is valuable as people from different backgrounds make unique contributions to any program.

Discontinuity can be as complicated as it is valuable. A director told us the following story about hiring a male teacher.

A Place to Wrestle

I always wanted to implement a gender-neutral curriculum—well, as close as possible. Yet lots of assumptions can be unpacked when I reflect upon my decision to hire a male teacher. I assumed a male teacher would be good for diversity of gender. I was so excited that he had an early childhood degree! During the first week of school he asked to buy a mattress for his classroom. Sure, I thought, he wants to create a cozy literacy area. He is early childhood degreed, so he will implement "best practice."

Instead, he placed the mattress in the middle of the room and established a wrestling area. To me, facilitating wrestling between 3-year-olds was not best practice. I was taken aback and realized I was making lots of assumptions—about good environments, best practices, and the gendered ways these can play out in the classroom.

This director hoped the addition of a male teacher would challenge traditional gender stereotypes. She knew that teachers influence children's developing notions of gender (Aina & Cameron, 2011). Instead, he enacted a "gendered" male experience in the classroom. The director was shocked by his decision but told us that she supported it once she reflected on this:

> I *was* lessening gender stereotypes by hiring a male teacher but did
> not want him to be stereotypically male in his gendered practices.
> I was unaware that my expectation was that this male teacher
> would behave like most early childhood teachers—practices rooted
> in stereotypical female activities—because we are a gendered
> profession.

Inspired to learn more about how other early childhood professionals experience continuity and discontinuity, we began the process of researching continuity. We read about it, talked to others about it, and in this book we are sharing the findings that emerged from this process.

Existing Conversations About Continuity

The concept of continuity appeared in educational literature about a century ago with roots reaching at least as far back as the 1920s, when Samuel Parker and Alice Temple encouraged continuity between kindergarten and 1st grade (Scully, Seefeldt, & Barbour, 2003). It has reappeared since then in different ways (Mayfield, 2003; Noddings, 1991; Sullivan, 2012; Wood & Bennett, 1999). *Continuity* can refer to the shape of a child's developmental trajectory and it can connect two separate individuals, entities, or ways of being.

Developmental Continuity. Often, ideas about continuity are based on child development research that is greatly influenced by the work of Arnold Gesell (1943). Developmental continuity describes the gradual forward-moving changes in growth that occur over time. The belief that development is "sequential and hierarchical" (Scully, Seefeldt, & Barbour, 2003, p. 11) leads to practices that promote continuity and attempt to minimize discontinuity in an otherwise forward-moving developmental trajectory. For example, teachers design spaces and experiences to match and enhance children's development. They select furniture that fits the children's physical development. Chairs in a classroom for 2s are typically smaller than in a classroom for 3s. Knowing that friendships are of prime importance to most 4-year-olds, teachers plan opportunities for children to work on projects together in small groups.

On the other hand, developmental systems theorists maintain that development is not a progression of individual behaviors but "arises within a context as a result of multiple developing elements" that are mutually interdependent (Thelen, 1995, p. 82). It occurs in uneven spurts and does not always follow a forward-moving progression. This view of development requires that teachers observe children carefully and nonjudgmentally. The infant who has already taken first steps may choose to crawl instead for a while. The toddler who breezily waves good-bye to dad one morning may be in tears the next.

Such differences in beliefs about the nature of development result in differing perceptions of continuity in daily practice. The first establishes continuity as unquestionably desirable. The second asserts the role of both continuity and discontinuity in development. What emerges is no longer a single perception of developmental continuity.

An ideal of developmental continuity and a forward-moving developmental trajectory can come into conflict with continuity between home and school. For instance, despite its current emphasis on respect for home cultures, Head Start was initially designed as a compensatory program that redirected the child's development. The thought at the time was that, left uninterrupted, the child's development would fall short of optimal. A program such as Head Start would alter the developmental trajectory as families took on more teacher-like attitudes and values and teachers provided optimal learning environments for children outside the home (Peters & Kontos, 1987). In the case of children living in poverty, the designers and implementers of Head Start valued discontinuity for averting what they considered diminished developmental growth for the child. Pressure on teachers, children, and families to move children along a developmental continuum that maximizes their growth potential continues today and can work against another type of continuity, continuity between home and school, specifically, cultural continuity.

Cultural Continuity. Culturally responsive education strives for continuity between the child's experiences in the home and in the early childhood program (Neuman & Roskos, 1994). In programs that are culturally congruent with children and their families, teachers understand that cultural beliefs, norms, and values guide behavior and expectations for themselves and the families and children with whom they work. They support each child's continued growth and development with efforts to understand children in their family contexts and have open and ongoing dialogue with families. Educators also learn from colleagues and community members as we hear in the next story.

Subtle Things You Can't Teach

You call someone by her last name ("Mrs. Jones") the deeper into the community she is and by her first name ("Ms. Bertha") if she does not have that status. There are people here I've always called by their last name, aides and assistant teachers. It's not their status within the system; it's their status within the community. These are the subtle things you can't teach anybody.

This director's explanation of the use of titles—when to and when not to use first or last names while addressing teachers at her school—provides evidence of how intricate cultural continuity is. People do not earn these titles because of their position at the school but rather from their status within the local cultural community. No one explicitly taught the director about appropriate titles. Most likely, she learned about them from observing over time.

The Regional Educational Laboratories' Early Childhood Collaboration Network (1995) defines a goal of continuity in this way: "[for] families to be able to shape and choose appropriate services for themselves and for their young children at every step along their path" (p. 9). Cultural discontinuity between home and school means that schools and families have to find new ways to work together in order to achieve this goal.

As children move through school, they continue to transition between home and school but also transition across multiple school settings, ranging from child care to preschool and on into the public school K–12 system. Fearing a lack of continuity between these education settings, recent scholarship has focused on building structural continuity within and across educational settings and levels.

Structural Continuity. Policies, rules, common practices, and regulations attempt to establish structural continuity. This occurs when children move between settings that share such qualities as teacher–child ratio, numbers of children per class, credentialing requirements, salaries, and licensing and other regulations (Kagan, 1991). Educators and researchers who believe that abrupt change or discontinuity is unhealthy for the child have sought ways to smooth children's transitions between settings, grade levels, and systems. Fabian and Dunlop (2002) found that as children make the transition between programs that differ structurally, the social competence, problem-solving skills, and sense of agency they used, for example, in child care may or may not serve them well in their kindergarten. Some schools hope to create continuity for children from pre-K to 3rd grade by aligning practices across the ages and making special efforts to smooth the transition. These include "consistency in learning environments, program quality, coordination and integration of curriculum and teaching practices, and family support services" (Geiser, Horowitz, & Gerstein, 2013, p. 2).

In addition, Lombardi (1992) calls for continuity across early care and education programs. She advocates adherence to developmentally appropriate practices for children, asserting that if all early childhood programs followed them, children would experience consistency as they progressed through programs over the years.

While Lombardi talks about aligning curriculum practices, the scope of continuity in current early childhood policy ranges beyond curriculum alone. For example, in 2007 the National Early Childhood Accountability Task Force called for continuity between early childhood institutions and agencies and public schools. The authors of this policy paper offer recommendations to enhance continuity in accountability and improvement efforts from the preschool years through grade 3. They ask state leadership to set the stage for early childhood and elementary school educators to work together in reviewing assessment data and in using the findings to strengthen teaching, learning, and professional development efforts. As educational reformers apply continuity more broadly, they link it to accountability. Fonthal (2004) maintains:

> Standards-based systemic school reform in the United States considers the alignment of the public schooling system as a desired goal that would ensure an efficient and effective educational system. Alignment and continuity among standards, assessments, curriculum, professional development, and pedagogy is, then, considered a condition for a healthy school system, and ultimately a condition for student success. (p. 1)

However, this type of continuity within and across educational settings is not the only view education scholars promote. Cagliari (2012) instead embraces a view of learning that is web-like and sometimes unpredictable, suggesting that teachers can establish continuity of learning across grades if they begin with what each child knows, perhaps intuitively, and progress outward, in a spiral, toward more abstract concepts using the child's narratives. The teacher documents children's knowledge acquisition over the year in relation to required curriculum; however, the child's knowledge, not standards or benchmarks, drives curriculum. This notion of continuity, grounded in a constructivist view of the child in charge of learning, stands in stark contrast to aligning and perhaps standardizing curriculum and pedagogy.

The desire to build continuity into early childhood curriculum across diverse contexts and programs is not without its challenges. Wood and Bennett (1999) conclude that even when mandated at a policy level, continuity and progression are difficult to achieve because (1) current outcomes-based policies reflect an overly simplistic view of learning that contrasts with professional recognition that learning is a complex process, (2) more research is needed to understand how educators transform educational policy into classroom curriculum, and (3) there is a lack of understanding of how teacher's theoretical orientations affect the pedagogy.

Continuity in early childhood thus applies to developing individuals; their relationships with the adults in their lives as well as to connections between home and school; the programs between which children transition; and to the flow of people, data, and practices across the larger educational system. Throughout, practitioners and policymakers seem to regard continuity as generally desirable, yet it remains difficult to achieve and relatively unexamined.

New Conversations

After reading about continuity, we began asking early childhood practitioners and parents from across the country to share their stories of continuity and discontinuity. We attended local, national, and international conferences and presented sessions on continuity, during which we asked participants to share stories with us about continuity. We then considered how those stories intersected with research on continuity. We spoke one on one and in small groups with parents, extended family members, teachers, administrators, home visitors, developmental specialists, university professors, students who are preservice teachers, and more. Some wrote their stories. Others told them to us. Some shared one story; others had many to share. Each story's author provided written consent.

The stories tell of programs in affluent areas; in places where families live in poverty; in urban, suburban, and rural communities. They reflect the lives of families and the work of individuals associated with university lab schools, family child care homes, Head Start programs, private programs, public schools, and community health organizations.

When we requested stories about continuity or discontinuity, the storyteller often asked what the terms meant, but we resisted defining them, to hear what they meant to each individual. Every story added a dimension to our understanding of the terms.

In these stories *continuity* meant sameness, congruence, coherence, connection, familiarity, predictability, comfort, or safety and was based on communication. We also heard continuity described as the status quo. The following is an example.

You Don't Really Know

I know that I am not the only early childhood educator who does not have kids of my own, but I have always felt like parents expected me to be a parent, too. It's as if having children creates continuity with the role of someone who cares for children, and not being a parent makes me an outsider. I usually don't disclose my personal situation, but sometimes people ask me directly. And sometimes when I admit that "no, I don't have children myself," they say, "Then you don't really know, do you?"

As in this story, the storytellers often, though not always, referred to discontinuity as the opposite of continuity. Stories about discontinuity included difference, incongruence, being out of sync, the unknown, mystery, novelty or newness, discomfort, exciting challenges, and fear-inducing challenges. As you will see in the chapters that follow, the landscape of stories was vast. A seemingly simple and unquestioned concept, continuity, is, in fact, far more complex than we had imagined.

Each story expanded the breadth of our work on continuity. As researchers we read and reread the stories and discussed the themes. We categorized the stories and integrated them into the chapters that follow. The themes that emerged from the stories became a framework for understanding what others have written. New questions and ideas arose as we looked closely at the concepts of continuity and discontinuity to understand their impact on us as families and as teachers and other education professionals.

Taken together, what we read in the literature and learned from individuals' personal stories demonstrated how continuity is frequently both a buzzword and a positive trait. Yet because the stories also illustrate the lived contexts in which continuity plays out, we see that "best practices" do not always reflect what is best for children and families in all programs and settings.

CONTINUITY AND EARLY CHILDHOOD PRACTICE

As you read the stories in this book and consider what they mean to your practice, we hope your reflection will deepen your thinking about continuity and discontinuity in education. Every teacher experiences both.

Teachers interact daily in continuous and discontinuous ways with children, families, and colleagues. At the same time, they live with policies, some of which aim to create continuity. Continuity and productive discontinuity depend on the relationships that result from, and sometimes in spite of, the framework policies create.

We conclude this introduction with a tour of the chapters that are yet to come. Continuity and discontinuity permeate early childhood education, as you will see as you read the remaining chapters.

Practices, Policies, and Relationships

Continuity is not a practice or policy but rather results from the nature of interactions that can (but do not necessarily) happen as part of a practice or because of a policy. Policies can set rules but cannot guarantee the results of their implementation. A director told us the following.

Lived Experience

We treat our teachers as professionals. They attend many training events; they keep records about the children; they work together on curriculum and classroom environments. We ask the teachers, as early childhood professionals, to provide child-centered early childhood education that may or may not fit with their lived experience. Their professional lives may be discontinuous with their personal lives.

Policies can dictate that teachers obtain at least a bachelor's degree or attend a certain number of hours of professional training. But as this story indicates, when the values embedded in training and education conflict with the core of who teachers are, the requirement cannot guarantee that the teachers will embrace or enact the pedagogy they learn in college or at workshops. Teachers can hear that children need to explore and take risks but may not allow children to climb up the slide. No matter how convincing a training session may be, they are likely to stick with what they learned as young children or to adhere to their own practice as parents. They maintain continuity with their backgrounds while policies strive for philosophical continuity across programs.

Continuity and discontinuity depend on the people involved. They hinge on children, families, and professionals and on the spaces in which they interact. In addition, each person's past experiences and individual differences influence any encounter. The stories that fill the following pages reveal the relational nature of continuity and discontinuity for anyone working with children and families.

The relational nature of continuity has an impact on individuals as they move in and out of communities and cultural contexts and interact with the people, values, and traditions within those contexts. With that in mind, this book turns frequently to the work of Urie Bronfenbrenner (1979) and examines continuity and discontinuity as they exist within an ecological system. Bronfenbrenner's ecological system is a nested one that begins with the individual at the innermost point. From there, concentric circles show how the ecology expands outward through different systems. These include family, work, and community, as well as governmental, cultural, and economic systems. People move back and forth between systems. The systems shape them and they, in turn, influence the systems.

In the pages that follow, we consider the ecological system to understand continuity and discontinuity. We use Bronfenbrenner's theory of an ecological system to explore the interplay of different levels. Decisionmakers develop policies and best practices at the macro level, but educators are to implement them at the micro level. That most local level is where children, families, teachers, and other professionals reside and experience the effects of policies.

What Is Yet to Come

Chapter 2 begins with the experience of the individual child, who is at the center of the ecological system. Continuity of care is itself a system to create continuity for children, and this chapter examines it and other practices that connect teachers to children and their families. In this chapter we question—from the perspective of the child, teacher, family, and center—why educators may or may not want to practice continuity of care. We discuss attachment, developmental continuity, and the role of continuity in children's developing self-regulation. Throughout this chapter, stories of real experiences both confirm and question commonly held beliefs about continuity of care.

In Chapter 3 we explore continuity between home and school and theories that advocate for home-school continuity. We offer multiple views of continuity between home and school and consider why continuity between home and school may be desirable and, when there is discontinuity, who accommodates whom to create the desired continuity. We discuss new ways to conceptualize continuity as we probe the impact of relational continuity on continuity between home and school. This chapter paints a vivid picture of the challenges families and professionals confront as they come together, enabling the reader to consider how to respond and how to advocate for children and families in the face of similar situations.

Chapter 4 expands the focus on continuity beyond the teacher, child, and family. We examine the most macro level, that is, contemporary policies and practices that attempt to create an early childhood system that improves quality by creating continuity. This chapter introduces the reader to policies in development and the types of initiatives that federal, state, and local governments fund with the expectation that they will create continuity for the child, family, and larger educational system. We explain what an early childhood system is and how educators develop one. Stories from families and professionals who interact within those systems demonstrate how policies and procedures enacted at a macro level affect individuals at the micro level. This chapter takes questions we raised in Chapters 2 and 3 to a national scale. Importantly, this chapter helps the reader see how continuity and discontinuity can be misconstrued and inappropriately used to justify standardizing practices.

Chapter 5 moves from this expanded conversation to return the focus to the individual—the educator. Here we consider early childhood identities. Through educators' stories, we investigate continuity and discontinuity within these identities. We also look at what factors contribute to that continuity and discontinuity. Importantly, we query how issues of power and powerlessness contribute to feelings of continuity and discontinuity in early childhood educators' identities. By examining this complex interplay of concepts and contexts readers can consider the identities they hold and how notions of continuity have shaped those identities.

We conclude the book in Chapter 6 with the story of one program and how it evolved. This story demonstrates how continuity and discontinuity at every level—individual, interpersonal, and systemic—play out in the daily life of early childhood educators. Since this is not a book with definitive conclusions, this final chapter raises key questions for readers to apply to their ethical, reflective, and evolving practice. Together, these chapters generate a broad and complex view of continuity and discontinuity.

CHAPTER 2

Continuity of Care
Where the Work of Early Childhood Is

Like a Homecoming

I work at a center that practices continuity of care. Each classroom has two head staff. In the infant-toddler-2s classrooms, one teacher always moves with the children. Often one stays behind to work with the "new" teacher. I have worked with infants several years in a row, worked with toddlers several years in a row, and also moved from infants to toddlers to 2s with a group of children and their families. Our 3s to 5s stay in the same class with at least one head teacher during all their preschool years. After the summer, it's not such a shock coming back. It's a wonderful experience for the child and the staff to return. What makes it wonderful are the relationships and the trust, the communication and comfort that are built up. It's like a homecoming.

Continuity of care as we define it is a conscious effort to attend to the flow of a child's experience in early care and education settings. Often, when people think of continuity of care, they think of infants and toddlers. Lally and Signer (n.d.) say it means each child has one primary caregiver from the time she enters child care until she is 3. The teacher telling the story above defines *continuity of care* to mean that children remain with some of the same teachers and children for an extended period of time—at least for more than one year. Children may be in a mixed-age group, starting out as the youngest and gradually becoming among the oldest. Alternatively, they may be with children their age who have at least one consistent adult, perhaps moving to a different classroom to have materials and equipment that fit their most recent developments. Everyone agrees that for continuity of care to work, the group must be small enough to allow the staff to get to know children well.

The teacher we quote at the start of this chapter and many others who spoke to us about continuity of care talked about relationships, trust, communication, and comfort. In fact, "close, ongoing relationships" in the child's life (Lally & Signer, n.d., p. 1) are at the core of continuity of care. Warm and loving relationships feel good to everyone

17

(Baker & Manfredi/Petitt, 2004), but very young children—infants who are just discovering the world of objects—depend on their relationships with others as they come to know themselves and their surroundings (Stern, 1985).

Lally and Signer's definition of continuity of care emphasizes the structures in which relationships have time to develop as children and adults grow and change together. Trust can build as they get to know one another. Communication can be easier with people who know each other well. Finally, the predictability and reliability of the setting and the people in it can create a comfortable environment for children, families, and teachers. For the teacher above, who works in a university-based program, continuity of care creates "a homecoming" each time children, families, and staff return to the group.

In this chapter, teachers and families describe continuity of care as they experience it. Some discuss why they and the children thrive on it, and others explain why they have trouble with it. All these stories help us examine what continuity of care is, what complicates it, and what issues it raises for educators.

THE MACRO AND MICRO LEVELS OF CONTINUITY OF CARE

Continuity of care has two dimensions. On the one hand, it is a set of structures that policies can establish. On the other, it is about relationships. While policies can facilitate relationships, they cannot guarantee that the relationships form and deepen. A director we spoke to referred to these two dimensions as the macro and micro levels.

In this section we look at the structures that make up the macro level. Then we examine what this director says about the micro level and the attention to detail and other factors involved in relationships between teachers and children and their families.

Structural Mechanisms that Sustain Continuity of Care

The Macro Level

The program I am at now, which has always understood the importance of continuity, has been pressured to get bigger, but we've resisted. So much of what we do has to do with staying small. Babies develop relationships with peers and teachers, and those people follow them into the toddler room and then into the preschool room. There are many teachers who have been with the same children since they were 3 months old. We build enormous continuity into how the program runs. That's the macro level of continuity.

Three structural mechanisms in addition to small group size sustain continuity of care at the macro level: primary caregiving, mixed-age grouping, and looping.

   Primary Caregiving. Picture a group of eight infants and three teachers. Each child has one primary caregiver who comes to know the child and family well. The primary caregiver is the main person caring for that child outside the home, constantly keeping that baby's developmental progress in mind and speaking to the family about the child. The team may assign primary caregivers randomly before children start or may decide after making home visits. Caregivers may already have "primaries" from the previous year, and the choice of a new primary may rest on the age of the new child. In this center, each staff member has either two or three primaries. While the others know the child, too, the primary caregiver is "ultimately accountable for the baby" (Raikes & Edwards, 2009, p. 81). The other caregivers become the baby's extended family; in some programs they only diaper her, for example, when her primary caregiver is unavailable. Primary caregiving usually becomes less intensive as the baby develops.
   When we asked a caregiver for a story about continuity, she described her relationship with one of her primaries.

Emotional Security

When I first started, she was a breastfed baby and had a hard time adjusting to being away from her mom. She cried whenever she saw an unfamiliar face. I got her at 6 months. Now she's almost 2, and she's doing so much better. Before, she was not interacting with her peers. Now she interacts with peers, with adults, even with strangers. She seems happier. She built a relationship with us, and we built one with her. She became more secure and more comfortable as time went on. Once this child was secure emotionally, everything else fell into place, and she was able to learn. Before, she was doing a lot of crying, and we couldn't engage with her. Now, we can read her stories and do activities that help her learn.

   This breastfed baby was accustomed to face-to-face nurturing moments with her mom. When she started Early Head Start at 6 months, primary caregiving facilitated her transition to group care. Although her caregiver could not replicate the experience of breastfeeding, she could look into the baby's eyes as she fed her a bottle and build on the baby's existing expectations of loving care.

According to Bowlby's attachment theory, infants take in the way adults treat them and come to anticipate that kind of interaction (Bretherton & Mulholland, 2008). They develop an internal working model and, as they form and engage in social relationships, can refer to a pattern of interactions that is fixed inside them. If children anticipate that adults are available and ready to help them, they are more likely to take the risk of exploring new people, places, and things.

With primary caregiving, this baby continued to form her expectations of relationships as she learned about one new person. She developed a secondary attachment to her caregiver that supported, complemented, and did not compete with her enduring relationship with her mother (Goldstein, Hamm, & Schumacher, n.d.). The emotional foundation the family laid at home and that the center supported led to engagement in learning activities.

In most cultures, children develop attachments to more than one adult during the 1st year of life. Babies become attached to whoever spends time with them, is responsive to and emotionally engaged with them, and remains with them over time. Although children can develop attachments to several people, they seem to become more closely attached to some than to others. According to Bowlby, they develop a hierarchy of attachments (Cassidy, 2008). For example, they find it harder to separate from some of the people to whom they are attached than from others. Early childhood educators are part of that hierarchy, establishing themselves as secondary attachment figures while supporting the child's primary attachments.

Talking about her evolving views about primary caregiving, a teacher told us about an intake interview with a mother during which the teacher described primary caregiving. The teacher reported:

> [The parent's] face literally fell. When I asked her what the matter was, she said, "The reason I chose child care instead of a nanny is because I don't want my child to be as close to another person as my child is to me." We went back and forth awhile before she understood, but she needed reassurance that I would never get so close that I would replace her. That made me think about where and why primary caregiving was used. It began with children in an orphanage who had no parents. I realized that if I were a parent, I wouldn't be so thrilled about it either.

This teacher refers to René Spitz's work in Romanian orphanages after World War II, where infants who were separated from their parents for an extended period withered without maternal care. Recent research (Nelson, Fox, & Zeanah, 2014) confirms Spitz's findings. Yet in child care, a primary caregiver joins the child's hierarchy of attachments without replacing the child's primary attachment with the parent.

For this structure to work, the primary caregiver develops rapport with the family. Then, the caregiver can support the relationship between parent and child, observing them together, paying attention to parental concerns, and collaborating to find solutions. The family and caregiver share their observations and inform each other about the child's experiences at home and in the program. The caregiver respects the family's preferences, creating continuity between home and school and opening the door for conversations when discontinuities emerge (National Infant and Toddler Child Care Initiative, 2010).

This continuity depends on a commitment to relationships. A director told us about a program that did not acknowledge babies' existing relationships. As they transitioned to a new room, problems arose:

> not only for the children, but for their parents. The parents didn't trust either. They didn't know these teachers. They weren't deeply connected to them as the people who were helping to raise their children. And there was constant tension. Constant friction.

Relationships that develop over time and build trust are as important for the adults involved as they are for children. You will read more about relationships with families and continuity and discontinuity between home and school in the next chapter.

Mixed-Age Grouping and Looping. Mixed-age grouping and looping are two programmatic mechanisms that keep children and teachers together for more than 1 year (Casper & Theilheimer, 2010). Mixed-age group settings include children of different ages, and each child has the continuity of a 2- or 3-year experience with the same adults and at least some of the same children.

In looping, teachers move from age group to age group or from grade to grade with the same children. "Homecoming" described how infant-toddler caregivers looped with their children. A kindergarten teacher may loop with her class, becoming their 1st-grade teacher and then their 2nd-grade teacher. The children and teachers come to know each other well, and, at the start of each new school year, they save time ordinarily spent familiarizing the class with routines and assessing previous learning.

When a group of children, teachers, and families remain together for more than a year, trust can build and relationships can flourish.

That's what happened for this preschool teacher for whom looping was a new experience.

The Graduation

I got these children when they were 3 years old, and we just had our preschool graduation. They've gone through this process of getting older together. As a teacher, I found it's much more fun when you know the children and parents so well.

I asked them what they wanted graduation to look like. They picked their songs and movements. They decided they needed costumes. They had a lot of ideas. We took a trip to the fabric store, and they made costumes. Of course, their parents were dressing them in totally adorable clothes for the graduation, but they wanted to wear these costumes. They decided what they wanted for their performance. Some of them really wanted to dance. Each dancer had a moment to dance on her own. We called these solos. We also made blocks, and the kids who didn't take dance solos were builders. They all participated, because they were doing something they were proud to do.

I've been teaching for 6 or 7 years now, and this was the first time I've allowed the children to have that much freedom in deciding what we did for graduation. I trusted them and felt comfortable letting them have ownership. Also, I knew the parents so well that I knew they trusted us to make it work.

We have 24 preschoolers, and we had over 90 people at the graduation. The children had been together in infant and toddler care, too, and have such deep relationships. I don't think it would have been like that if they had not been together all those years. Together, they learned social-emotional-wise and their academic stuff, too. They really care about each other.

At our center the families range from affluent to homeless. They are all friendly with each other. Parents care about each other's kids, too. As a surprise to the teachers, a parent who is homeless stood up at graduation and made a speech thanking all the teachers. This parent had a hard time trusting us at first. I don't think she would have walked away with such a positive feeling after just 1 year. The amount of time together just makes such a big difference. It takes so long to feel comfortable, especially for the parents. After all, you're taking care of their children. Not to say that there aren't rougher parts of continuity of care, but in my experience it was great.

As you have seen, the structures of continuity of care, primary caregiving, mixed-age groups, and looping create spaces for relationships to develop. They do not guarantee those relationships, however. The next section discusses the components of relationships that are integral to achieving the purposes of continuity of care.

The Work of Developing Relationships

The director who spoke to us about the macro and micro levels of relationships added further comments as follows.

The Micro Level

The micro level is the baby's experience of continuity over the course of the day. We try to make it as seamless as we can. I always try to think about the child's day from the moment they open their eyes in the morning to when they close them again at night. My goal is to make that day make sense to the child. It doesn't seem a lofty goal, but when you are talking about a group care situation, it is quite a task sometimes. It takes thought and attention to details that some people would call anal. But it's not anal to an infant. It takes a flow of information among the adults for life to make sense to children. It's all the little things. The minutiae of life. That is the world children are attending to and if we want to do our jobs well, we'd best attend to it, too, for life to make sense for children.

This director is not dismissing the structures that keep children and teachers together for several years, but she emphasizes that continuity requires people who both care for and about the children in their group. To develop relationships with children, adults have a daily presence and attend to the details of children's days, recognize children's agency, support attachments, and maintain communication between adults. What are the minutiae or small details that make up an infant's daily life? How might attention to one of those details build your relationship with a child?

Daily Presence. When continuity of care goes beyond merely implementing structures, the adults are fully present. Adults are alert to children's verbal and nonverbal signals and cues, interact with children in a focused way, and mentally catalog their ongoing learning about each child. Their interactions with children are neither distracted nor dispassionate. Instead, these adults are fully engaged. The regularity of their daily presence makes them physically reliable, and the way in which they give of themselves makes them emotionally responsive.

The collaborative team of the American Academy of Pediatrics, the American Public Health Association, and the National Resource Center for Health and Safety in Child Care and Early Education advocates a "relationship-based philosophy" (2014, p. 36), and lists six caregiver behaviors that establish and support secure relationships between caregivers and children:

    a. Hold and comfort children who are upset
    b. Engage in frequent, multiple, and rich social interchanges such as smiling, talking, touching, singing, and eating;
    c. Be play partners as well as protectors;
    d. Be attuned to children's feelings and reflect them back;
    e. Communicate consistently with parents/guardians; and
    f. Interact with children and develop a relationship in the context of everyday routines (diapering, feeding, etc.).

These components make up what the caregiver who told the following story refers to as "our daily presence."

Becoming a Security Blanket

When this infant first came, she wouldn't eat. She cried. One of us had to hold her all the time. She was tense, and we did baby massage with her. She started moving and then crawling and growing. When she saw a stranger, she would cry hysterically until the person left. Now she's 1 year old and says "hi" and gives a high five. If she shies away from someone, she'll come to one of us as a security blanket. This child's adjustment has a lot to do with our daily presence. We work with her one on one and provide her with different experiences. If we leave the building or go outside, she backs up behind one of us, and we lift her up.

Simple presence, having adults in the room with the child, is not enough. Continuous, relationship-based, responsive care leads this caregiver, in her words, to become a child's "security blanket."

Responsive caregiving involves "prompt, consistent and sensitive reactions to an infant's distress on the part of its caregiver" (Maxwell & Racine, 2012, p. 161). To be responsive, the caregiver observes a baby to get to know her, reads her signals, and interacts with her in ways that respect the baby's (usually nonverbal) messages. Responsive caregivers are dependable, and babies come to trust them as reliable. They focus on the baby and are totally available and ready to respond (Gonzalez-Mena & Eyer, 2012). The caregiver who told the previous story seemed to find responsive caregiving gratifying, because it enabled her to watch the child relax, grow, and develop in her care.

Attention to the Details of Children's Daily Life. In infant-toddler care, caregiving routines provide many opportunities to build relationships if adults pay close attention to these details of daily life (Gonzalez-Mena & Eyer, 2012). Adults can imagine the child's experience as they help children fall asleep and wake up, sit with children as they eat and hold them as they drink a bottle, talk to them about their explorations on a mat or in motion, and diaper them or take them to the toilet. When adults take the child's perspective, they better understand and appreciate the child, and their relationship grows.

Older children often articulate what they experience and how they feel about it. Nonetheless, all teachers benefit from careful observation that seeks the child's point of view. When they record, share, and look back on those observations, teachers can reflect on and begin to understand children's experiences in new ways.

Sensitive teachers pay attention to the continuities and discontinuities that a child experiences, as did the following infant caregiver. Her observations illustrate how the child finds continuities that his teacher scaffolds.

James Explores Baby Play

One day in December, 13-month-old James made his way over to the library area where we have dolls of different ethnicities, including two small cloth Hawaiian dolls, Lei and Kalani, and two small doll-size blankets. James began "reading to Kalani." Later that month, James continued his baby play by swaddling Kalani, holding him for 10 minutes, and then "reading" a book to him. As I moved a bit closer, James lay Kalani down, and I began singing softly, describing what I saw James doing. He continued to hold and care for Kalani, walk away, and return.

In February, James began transitioning to the pre-toddler room. I went with him as I do for all the children during the initial days of the transitioning. I noticed that he was interested in the dolls with real eyes that moved. He picked one up and wrapped it and began carrying it around the room. His new teachers and I discussed ways to support this interest as he began his transition.

At 15 months, James visited his former infant room and immediately went to the library area. He saw Kalani and took the doll, wrapped him, patted him, and began advanced babbling. He was content.

Today, James is still a compassionate and caring child. As mobile infants transition to the pre-toddler room, he is quick to comfort ones that are upset, patting them on the back with a special hug. Some people call this altruism; it might be. I just know that on some days you can see James isolating himself from that busy toddler room and sitting near the edge of the library area holding a doll and a blanket.

James's teacher was sensitive to his need for continuity as he transitioned to a new classroom. She went with him to his new room, conferred with his new teachers, and welcomed his return visits. Her observations of James reveal the continuity he created for himself through his choice of activity. Her attention to the details of his day helped her to see how he dealt with discontinuity and change and how he comforted himself and others.

Recognizing Children's Agency. James's teacher also demonstrated her regard for him and his choices. Honest relationships with children are built on respect for and willingness to listen to children's intentions and desires, whether they have verbal language yet or not.

In the following case, a parent who is also an early childhood educator described her daughter Annie as having a "slow-to-warm temperament." Temperament is a combination of preferences and behavior patterns based on the degree to which an individual has each of nine traits (Thomas, Chess, & Birch, 1970, as cited in Fogel, 2009). For example, how much daily regularity and what activity level does he prefer? How much and under what conditions can he focus attention?

Annie's mom said Annie needs "predictability and reliability—all those things that go with continuity of care—that's when you can see how great she is, how reasonable. When it's not, she's distressed and anxious, and you can't see how great she is then." Notice how Annie asserted her agency in this story and made clear that her relationship to a caregiver carried over from prior experience into a new classroom with new adults.

The Child's Choice

When Annie transitioned from the infant room to the toddler room, she was going to have a new teacher, Meg, who was and is a dear friend of mine. I was excited and was sure Meg would be Annie's primary caregiver. There were three teachers in the room, and one of them, Beth, had been with Annie in the infant room. On our 1st day, my husband, Annie, and I came for phase-in. When we were trying to leave I passed Annie to Meg, because I'm attached to Meg. But Annie wanted Beth, whom she knew from the infant room. I needed to respect her comfort level and need for continuity and allow that to dictate who her primary caregiver was going to be. It hit home for me as a professional how important continuity is, how it made other things easier for her. And that cemented the idea that continuity is so important.

Annie demonstrates the power of a relationship that continued over time. Her mother, too, had strong feelings about the primary caregiving relationship and wanted Meg to be her main contact. Still, she deferred to her child's preference. Just as this mother did, professionals can credit even very young children with the ability to make intentional choices. That respect for children is an essential element of continuity of care.

Supporting Attachments. Working attentively with a child and his or her family from early in the child's life can lead early childhood educators to know them well, develop secondary attachments with the child, and support the attachment a parent and child have to each other. When the family remains involved in the program over time and the staff and family sustain their relationships, everyone benefits, as Michelle's story suggests.

Circling the Wagons

There was no doubt that Michelle's father, Michael, loved Michelle, but he had a substance abuse problem that compromised her care. Whether Michelle was in foster placements or in her father's care, her teachers made her classroom a safe place for her. Along with the onsite caseworker, they reached out to whoever was caring for her and got to know them. They welcomed Mike and foster mothers alike into the classroom and shared Michelle's experiences there. They even became, with the permission of the family, a consistent presence at Michelle's court hearings, testifying at times about the importance of continuity and advocating for Michelle to stay at the center.

Slowly, over 2 years in the same classroom with the same teachers, Michelle began to catch up with her peers. She was exceptionally articulate and when teachers met her needs for consistency and warm understanding, she was able to make huge strides in all developmental areas even though her home life was still unpredictable at times.

At a pivotal court hearing when Michelle was 4 years old, Mike's parental rights were at stake. After his third release from prison, he petitioned the court for custody of his daughter. She had just settled into her latest foster placement with a family that wanted to adopt her.

In our city, the prime objective of Child Protective Services is the successful reunification of parents and their children. We understood the underlying premise but were not confident that it would work. Happily, we were wrong. Mike's love for his daughter and her attachment to him proved to be the one consistent aspect of their lives that would form the foundation of their success. Everyone, from teachers to social workers, circled the wagons around this fragile relationship to support, deepen, and strengthen it.

When Michelle went to kindergarten, she and her father became one of the first families to join our new evening program designed to meet the needs of families transitioning away from the intense social and academic supports of the center into the wider community. This proved especially helpful to Mike and Michelle. Michelle is 9 now, and she and her father have stayed together with no relapses of substance abuse or prison time. They still attend the evening program, and last year their caseworker helped prepare Mike for the plumber's license exam that would ensure his career. Life is not perfect for this little family; Michelle's social-emotional regulation still needs support. They have each other, though, and are strong together.

This story illustrates how relationships that developed as a result of continuity of care supported Michelle's attachment to her father. Within Michelle's larger picture of continuity and discontinuity, the program provided a continuous thread. The continuity of relationships with other children, with teachers, and with the program in general, well into Michelle's elementary school years, formed a vital core for both her and her father.

Maintaining Communication Between Adults. Teachers who care about relationships strive for open communication with children and families. Equally important are the relationships between the adults and the communication they have with each other. When teachers tell each other about the children, everyone can work as a team to make the children's day in a care and education setting a meaningful and seamless part of their overall experience. As one director said,

> All the adults involved have to have all the information to make decisions. If a child is in a horrible mood and only one person knows why, then the others can't make sense of the experience with the child. They can't narrate what's happened to the child. Everybody has to know each child's story. Daily. That's where the work of early childhood is. It's very hard to keep that going.

A story from another program highlights communication between adults in a classroom for 4-year-olds. A preschool director told us about a classroom where teachers collaborated to make the room work for one particular child.

Hidden and Invisible

There's a rhythm to the day. This is particularly important for one child who struggles during circle, story, or even free play. And transition time is hardest. Continuity and what's next is very important to this child. In addition, everyone on staff has to have continuity of practice with this particular child. We talked about how important it is to notify this child about what's going to happen. Everyone agreed we would inform him 5 minutes before anything changed.

Sometimes, however, communication does break down, to the detriment of continuity for children and their success in the group. When the lead teacher was out, the others did not communicate the plan to the substitute. The director continued,

> Because of the weather, part of the day was altered. The teachers explained to the children that they would have a story inside when they would normally go outside. All the children heard it except for this child, who was in the hallway returning from the bathroom.
> As the child entered the room and saw that there was a change, he had a meltdown. The environment was different from what he expected. The children were not getting their coats to go outside. It was a real lesson. Teachers got to see how the smallest thing—even things that are hidden and invisible and that we don't even think about—could create a huge disruption.

The breakdown in communication within the teaching team led to discontinuity of practice. When new adults enter the picture, they can join the effort only if the other teachers communicate what the group has agreed upon previously. Communication between adults is particularly critical for children who struggle with change.

Communication is also a necessary element of continuity when outside specialists work with individual children. Classroom teachers can maximize what children gain from those services when service providers and teachers communicate and collaborate.

While the structures of continuity of care are readily apparent, continuity itself can be invisible or at least hard to pinpoint and thus to replicate on a large scale. Yet continuity is important for children and teachers. The next section examines why.

THE IMPORTANCE OF CONTINUITY OF CARE

The previous sections discuss what continuity of care looks like and stress that it extends beyond a set of practices. The relationships that develop bring meaning to children's care and education experience and help them manage long hours away from home. In addition, continuity of care can be a source of professional fulfillment to the adults who work with them.

The Value of Continuity of Care for Children

Continuity of care and its inherent attention to children and respect for their agency support children's abilities. Children learn to expect that the adults at their program will care for and about them and will help them through difficult times. They become able to predict activities and, therefore, make choices more easily. They even become more able to regulate their own behavior.

   Relationships with Dependable Adults. As you have read, the primary caregiver takes responsibility for the child's care routines and for communication with the family. As the relationship between child and caregiver develops, the child learns to depend on the caregiver, and sometimes the strength of the relationship is apparent to outsiders, as in the next story.

Soothing

One day, a young toddler got his fingers pinched under the lid of the sensory table. A parent of another child was not far away. After she got his fingers out, she held him. He was not injured, but it was painful and he was crying. I called over the toddler's primary caregiver. As soon as the caregiver picked him up and held him, he was soothed. He nuzzled into her neck and stopped crying. I remember this so clearly, because the parent looked at me, her jaw dropped, and she said, "OMG, that was wild!" The toddler had continuity with this one woman at our center, and that was what was soothing to him.

   Something magical—or wild, as the parent looking on put it—happened when toddler and primary caregiver connected. Knowing the toddler, the primary caregiver could read him, even though he was not yet using words. Having an internalized sense of the caregiver's responsiveness, the toddler turned to her when he needed her. He knew she was dependable and would meet his expectations.

In the next story, a teacher came to know a preschool age child well while working with him for 3 years. The program did not have a policy of continuity of care or primary caregiving, but Ronnie and a few others remained in the teacher's class for more than a year. In this story, a caring and observant teacher met a child where he was and created a classroom community where other children treated him in the same way.

The Incidents of Connection

It took Ronnie a long time to move toward the group. He stayed at the periphery of the room. He entered the group by mucking about on the easel. Those were his first steps. The rest of the children sensed Ronnie was different, but they treated him like a person, not as a pet. He began to allow them to touch him before he allowed me to touch him. They would say, "You have to put your mittens on," and he'd flap his hands. They grabbed him and said, "Stay still," and he did it. And there was a glow of satisfaction on his face. He was being part of what was going on.

He imitated other children. It was the power of other children as role models. After a while he allowed another child to hold his hand as we walked to the playground. It was awkward. He'd hold up his hand and the other child would grab it. Part of his ability to become a group member, although never completely, was the "get with it" attitude of the other kids.

His observations of other children's interactions helped him to develop a relationship with me. At naptime, I'd wrap children in their blankets and rub their backs. Ronnie couldn't tolerate that. One day I was sitting on the floor and he began to flap his arms furiously but not angrily. He was trying to say something but couldn't get it out. I said, "Ronnie, do you want me to wrap you?" He grabbed his blanket from his cubby, flopped down into my lap, and cried for the first time, and I cried, too.

The continuity Ronnie had with his teacher and the rest of the class made discontinuities, in this case breakthroughs, possible. In our efforts to create continuity for children, we can forget the disruptive nature of development, how positive that discontinuity is, and the way in which it speaks to children's individual agency and to the agency of the group.

Ronnie's consistent relationship with his teacher led him to trust her. Throughout, she watched and listened for his nonverbal cues and had the acuity to read them and act upon them. His story reminds us to give children time to move at their own pace and learn when they're ready, which may be easier to do when a child is with the same teacher for an extended period of time.

Predictability. In preschools and elementary schools, classroom routines and schedules give children a modicum of control over classroom life. So, too, for very young children who experience the predictability of reliable relationships.

In the following story, a family member thinks about the relationship she developed with her niece for whom she was caregiver. She describes how her niece demonstrated that she remembered their experiences.

I Spent That Time with Her

Last year I spent time with my 16-month-old niece three times a week. We looked out the window, and I talked to her about what was going on outside, about the children, the trees, and the dogs. She also loved to play with plastic cups. She put one inside another. She put colorful heart-shaped pasta in a bottle and mixed them.

Now, after a year, when she comes over, she remembers. She can speak and says, "Children are coming back from school." She goes to the kitchen and points to the pasta container, showing me that she wants to play with it. She remembers it after a long time, probably because we did it a few times a week for a few months. She came over last Sunday and went to look out the window. Only I know why, because I spent that time with her.

The continuity of what they shared led this child to expect behaviors, experiences, and materials. Both child and adult find comfort in the predictability of their shared expectations.

Support for Self-Regulation. Self-regulation, the ability to monitor and manage one's behavior, contributes to children's positive interactions with others and exploration of their surroundings. Self-regulation is essential to getting along with others, particularly in a group. It also enables children to focus their attention and learn (Galinsky, 2010).

The ability to self-regulate develops, as the child does, through experiences with others. The child internalizes control as adults and other children explicitly communicate desirable behavior verbally and implicitly define what is acceptable through their actions. Very young children learn to self-soothe through experience and with help (the offer of a favorite soft toy, for example). As children grow older, they develop strategies for controlling their impulses. This difficult task demands the child's cognitive, physical, social, and emotional work and is thus a challenge that involves the whole developmental system (Casper & Theilheimer, 2010). The next story illustrates the connection between continuity of care and self-regulation.

Crashing and Loudness

A little girl in our pre-K class is hearing impaired and has Down syndrome. While she was on vacation, her one-to-one teacher left to take a new job. When the child returned to school, her one-to-one teacher wasn't there. We saw a decrease in the child's expressive and receptive communication; an increase in pushing limits; and an increase in behaviors she had previously outgrown, like dumping bins of materials, self-stimulation, and unintentional play. We see that with other children too. When there's discontinuity, their dysregulation behaviors increase. There's crashing, loudness. Continuity, predictability, and routine make our children feel more masterful. They know what to expect.

Continuity offers children security and comfort, a safe space from which to venture forth. Knowing what to expect, children have the wherewithal to deal with a painful or surprising situation, as you saw in "Soothing."

Discontinuity, especially in the form of novelty, on the other hand, stimulates and challenges children to roll over for the first time or figure out how to complete a puzzle. Yet discontinuity can disrupt a more fragile child's ability to manage. The child in "Crashing and Loudness" illustrates dysregulation. Her ability to play with intention and hold herself together began to crumble when her teacher's disappearance interrupted the regularities she had come to expect at school.

The Value of Continuity of Care for Teachers

Teachers also value continuity of care. They, too, experience the connection and the predictability of consistent, loving relationships. Continuity of care can give teachers a sense of self-efficacy, the feeling that they have done their job well. It affords them professional development opportunities. Continuity of care enhances the emotional quality of the job, which can be fulfilling and, at times, wrenching.

Sense of Self-Efficacy. Teachers appreciate the way continuity of care can help them to know children, as a 10-year teaching veteran's story illustrates.

Three Years to Cherish

For the past 3 years I have had the same children. We started out in 1st grade and ended our time together going into 4th grade. It was amazing what I accomplished with this group—from the students who could not read to the students reading way above a 1st-grade level. Starting out 2nd grade made everyone's heart fluffy 'cause we all knew what to expect. We said our hellos and started learning from day 1. All routines and structures were already in place, some reminders were given, but not much was needed.

The following year I had two groups in 3rd grade, each for half the day. We (the group I had for two previous years) started the year the same way. I knew which students lacked what concepts and where to start. The class made tremendous strides in all areas and levels. My only concern was the new group of children. I could not fully use the lesson plans I created for my continuing students. I realized the amount of positive outcomes from having the same kids for 3 years. I used the same lessons for the new group but taught with more detail, to fill in the gaps. I will start this coming year with excitement of what is to come, and I will cherish those 3 years always.

Since children and teachers knew one another and the classroom, they picked up where they had left off the previous year. Learning became continuous. The teacher taught more, children learned more, and the teacher felt more competent and effective as a result. If learning occurs in the context of relationships and within communities of learners (Rogoff, 1994), the "fluffy" hearts she mentions indicate that the continuity of looping with the children created a relational community for teacher and children alike, along with a professional experience for the teacher to "cherish."

Professional Development. Continuity of care is not without its challenges, however. As the next teacher says, it is, unlike more fleeting interactions, a long-term commitment to children, to families, and to relationships with them.

More of a Commitment

I stayed with the same children from kindergarten to 3rd grade. It was a long time ago, but I remember it well. Just that memory of those kids; I really did have a deeper relationship with them. During those 3 years, there was a dad I would have liked to say good-bye to, but I couldn't. I had to figure out how to form a relationship with him. Spending 3 years with these children and families forced me as a teacher to ask constantly, How can I do this better? Maybe there was more of a commitment. Then with some kids, I felt, we're working hard, but we're not getting where we need to be. But the next year, I realized, we're here! This experience helped me understand the fits and starts of development.

Whether for very young children or for older ones, continuity of care raises issues that stretch teachers. First of all, these issues propel teachers to solve interpersonal challenges. The inevitability of this teacher's relationship with the father forced her to find a way to work with him respectfully and effectively. Second, she saw learning evolve over time and gained the patience to allow that to happen. Third, she became knowledgeable, not just as a 1st-grade teacher, but also as a 2nd- and 3rd-grade teacher. The children's changes prompted her need to know more about what children are ready to learn.

The impact of the children's changes on the classroom and on their academic progress makes the teacher's learning about them immediately useful (Ackerman, 2008). This teacher's continually growing awareness of children's strengths and efforts led her to see their development beyond a series of steps in a textbook. She could experience their development, not as a straightforward trajectory but as a discontinuous path that lurches forward and back in often unpredictable ways (Rochat, 2001).

Just staying together for 3 years did not make her relationships with the children happen. She made efforts to get to know the children, to figure out what made sense for each child, and to find ways to work with children and families with whom she did not connect readily. The continuity of looping and mixed-age groups means that what is good continues and what is not so good may continue as well. As the professional, this teacher believes she bears the responsibility of making the relationships work. That and the many issues that arise with an ever-changing and diverse group of children create professional development opportunities for teachers.

Emotional Fulfillment and Challenges. Throughout this chapter, the voices of adults who work with children tell how fulfilling continuous, deep relationships with children can be. You hear teachers recall the joy of secure attachments and take pride in children's breakthroughs.

The depth of adults' feelings about the children with whom they work can make them especially vulnerable when inevitable discontinuities arise. In some cases, a continuity of care structure ironically forces separations. Some directors believe that early childhood educators develop expertise with one age group and want continuity for a classroom. As children transition to a toddler class, one caregiver remains in the infant room while another moves with the children. The children have the continuity of a known adult, as you saw when Annie selected Beth as her primary caregiver in the story "The Child's Choice." The center, in turn, has the continuity of an experienced infant teacher bringing new families into the program. That situation, however, is not without its costs, as the following story from a director illustrates.

How Teachers Feel

A teacher told me how difficult it was for her to spend a year developing relationships with infants and then have them leave for the toddler room. An assistant teacher from the infant room moved to the toddler room with the children, but this teacher remained in the infant room. She said it was painful for her to be unable to leave her new children to comfort the children she knew so well who were now in the toddler room.

Teachers' feelings enter into the relationships that continuity of care fosters. This program successfully juggled two competing interests: those of the children who had a familiar teacher with them in their new toddler room and those of the program itself that preserved an experienced presence in the infant room. A third interest, that of the infant teacher who remained to phase in a brand-new group, necessarily fell by the wayside. The depth of relationship between children and caregivers is something that the adults experience, too.

Thus, for teachers and children, continuity of care offers growth opportunities. Children can achieve more when they are secure and comfortable. Teachers can feel challenged and more productive. Continuity of care can engender close feelings, which have two sides—the warmth of their relationship and the sadness of separation. This hints at one reason why, despite the good reasons for continuity of care, some educators and parents argue against it.

REDEFINING AND RESISTING CONTINUITY OF CARE

For all its benefits, not everyone practices continuity of care. Some parents and educators believe that children thrive in a community of care, consider children flexible enough to sustain different relationships, or adhere to a developmental model that argues against aspects of continuity of care. Teachers' feelings enter into the equation as well. Some teachers prefer one age group over another, perceive status differences, or resist inevitable separations.

Beliefs About Children

Beliefs about children underlie decisions not to practice continuity of care. Believing firmly in a community of care, one may feel that primary caregiving overlooks or even undermines children's connection to many people at once. One may point to children's flexibility and resilience. In some cases, belief in developmental continuity leads adults to place children in a new environment as they reach a certain age or gain a new skill, such as walking.

A Community of Care. Primary caregivers work with the rest of their team to create a community of care for the children. Some programs, particularly those serving families from cultures in which relatives and close friends care for children along with the parents, may not implement primary caregiving. These families and program staff may believe in a community of care that takes advantage of the caregiving resources of all adults involved (Leinaweaver, 2014). The ideal then is for all the children to relate to all the adults. In non-Western cultures, in particular, infants often come to depend on many family and community members (Gottlieb, 2004). A director told us the following story.

A Collectivist Culture

I work primarily with African American families. The culture is much more collectivist. At the housing project where my previous center was, everybody's doors would open; children would come out, and someone would yell, "You're in charge!" to one person.

Also, when they went to church on Sunday, from infancy on, children were passed around. Infants would go to everyone the parent trusted.

Primary caregiving was counterintuitive to what I understood were the priorities of the culture. Primary caregiving speaks to a dyadic relationship, and I don't see relationships here as clearly dyadic as I see them in White middle-class culture. So, when I did use the primary caregiving system, I mainly used it as an intervention for a child who experienced trauma and really could use the experience of someone in the world to trust. And then, here we use a very modified version, because, to be honest, I don't think most of our teachers buy into primary caregiving.

Teachers who are from the program's neighborhood share families' preference that children become comfortable with multiple caregivers. The director, who is not of their culture, can identify and respect it, although she believes that continuity offers children stability that is valuable for children who regularly experience violence.

A mother told us that shortly after her child's birth, she opted for an au pair who lives with the family, someone from overseas who stays in the United States for no more than 18 months. As a result, in fewer than 5 years her child had five different au pairs or nannies.

Au Pairs

Our son is four now and our current au pair is the fifth we've had. The first was with us for a year and a half, the second for only 6 months, the third for another year and a half, and then one for only 6 months. Our current au pair started recently. We chose this form of child care because of our personal needs. From the time he was 6 weeks old, he's spent time regularly with multiple caregivers: an au pair, other babysitters, his grandparents, an adult cousin, and, of course, us, his parents. I think that's helped him. Even before he was old enough to understand, we talked to him about people coming and going. When anyone left, we celebrated her with a party. He also participated in Skype interviews with the au pairs. Most recently he thought of a question to ask the prospective au pair: "Do you like trains?" Our current au pair answered that she loves trains, and he chose her. Our first and third au pairs, who were each with us for a year and a half, have stayed in touch with us. Our son knows that when you say good-bye it's not the last time you'll see someone. I know about attachment and minimizing transitions, but I look at the flip side, too. Our son is more comfortable in new environments and accepting of new people as caregivers and teachers.

This mother seems to value her child's ability to be "more comfortable in new environments and accepting of new people as caregivers and teachers," and at the same time emphasizes that he has always had reliable, continuous attachments. While a variety of people cared for him, he was nonetheless able to develop confidence in a range of trustworthy people. The quality of the relationships trumps the discontinuity of separations (Zeanah, Anders, Seifer, & Stern, 1989).

A Climate of Care. One teacher told us that since most children are trusting and able to engage with any loving adult, the constant effort everyone makes to create a warm atmosphere and develop a relationship with every child is more important than continuity of care and primary caregiving.

Children Smile at Anybody

At our center it's a long day, so teachers come and go. The babies relate to many people, but teachers make intentional connections with them, and that makes the program work. Sometimes teachers travel with the children when they move to the next room, but, in any case, the babies are flexible and smile at anybody who treats them warmly. We have consistency among the teachers, and we're blessed with a 3:1 or 2:1 ratio of children to adults. We build relationships just through the daily reality of diapers and feeding, and we do value building those relationships. The center is our home; we're here every day. And we definitely focus on that moment. We model relationships. Children build relationships with each other. The staff has worked together enough years to have that feeling of home.

These teachers practice responsive caregiving and offer consistent care for and about children. Since it is an all-day program, children interact with various adults, all of whom respond to the children in the ways the children have come to expect. This program practices continuity of climate, using some of the structures of continuity of care. Their commitment to relationships accounts for the feeling of home.

Developmental Continuity. In the story "James Explores Baby Play" (p. 25), the program moved children from the infant room to the pretoddler room midyear. This and many other programs focus on children's ages and developments as such programs make decisions about placements. In many cases, programs hope to give each child an experience that matches the child's developmental stage. In some cases, though, changes are for the convenience of the program. A family moves away, and there is a slot in the 2s room. Moving a child "up" will fill it, and enrolling a new infant is easier than finding a new 2-year-old. In other cases, children are moved around the way a program has always placed children, without questioning the logic behind their practice.

While James's program helped him manage the transition, other programs may be less alert to children's experience. In either case, commitment to developmental continuity—to a belief that all children progress predictably according to ages and stages—drives a practice that can result in discontinuity of care. A director told us about her experience at a new job where children moved to another space once they reached 18 months.

Sent to the Other Side of the Gate

I worked in a program for infants and toddlers housed in one room separated into two spaces by a large baby gate. On one side was the infant room, which had children aged 6 weeks to 18 months, and on the other were the toddlers, who were 18 months to 3 years. This program, like many others, believed that to ensure a developmentally appropriate environment, at 18 months children should move to the toddler room on the other side of the baby gate. There they would have the materials, schedule, and activities appropriate to their age. It makes sense. But they forgot the people and the relationships.

This program chose to use its space to make sure that children received the learning environment they needed once they turned 18 months. Teachers seemed to subscribe to this practice, although the director did not.

> When I first entered the program, I was struck by how many children, especially the toddlers who had just "moved up," spent large parts of the day at the baby gate crying for the teachers who had cared for them since they were tiny. And the teachers pretended they didn't see them, or told them to go play. But these toddlers didn't want to play or talk or read books or sing. They used all their energy trying to understand why they were sent to the other side of the gate. Others who were not crying at the gate didn't seem to care. These "good adjusters" often had a marked lack of affect. They went where they were told, with whoever was there at the time. "Were these toddlers?" I asked myself. What about separation anxiety? What about attachment? I heard many times that children will get used to it. They're "resilient." And that may be true, but at what cost?
>
> When we ask something of children we must ask ourselves, "What are children's basic needs at this point?" If we are asking them to compromise those needs, how can we change our request?
>
> In this program, toddlers paid the price of social development. At snack time the children were feral, constantly shoving and grabbing and pushing. While well-attached toddlers are notorious for testing behavior, these children's behavior was more defensive and self-protective. They were confused and overwhelmed, with no confidence in the adults to meet their needs. They weren't checking in with an adult and weren't able to regulate themselves knowing an adult was there for them. No one knew them or could understand their language.

This program moved children into a room with materials that fit their age but that they could not use effectively, because the transition disarmed them emotionally. The teachers may have believed they were following developmentally appropriate practice. Yet they too seem to be protecting themselves emotionally. The story continues, with the director making a change to continuity of care. The emphasis now was on attachment theory and developmental systems theory rather than on developmental milestones.

When I made the changes, there was resistance from teachers. Teachers had built up their identity around their expertise. They didn't realize the stress they were putting on themselves by having to manage something so unnatural. Teachers finally said, "This does make sense. I can see myself as caring for this child instead of for this age group." Deep, connected relationships with children and families made them understand what this work really is.

Grouping children by age rests on the assumption that everyone in an age group shares characteristics. However, children do not develop at the same rate, and their development results from the dynamic interaction between their biological makeup and their experiences (Thelen, 1995). Focusing on relationships instead of developmental expectations turns teachers' attention to the children themselves and away from generalizations about a group.

Teachers' Feelings

This director's story opens a window onto the caregivers' feelings and worries. By doing what they had always done, teachers worked amid unhappy and disconnected children. At the same time, they remained in the comfort zone of the age group they knew. Her story provides a graphic illustration of how the discontinuity of a new age group, although with the same children, can create anxiety for a teacher.

A range of feelings accounts for teachers' resistance to continuity of care. They may prefer an age group. They may fear loss or even believe that an attachment with other people's children is wrong (Baker & Manfredi/Petitt, 2004). In the name of professional distance, they may avoid closeness with children and families.

Teachers' Specializations. In their research on four infant-toddler centers that claimed to practice continuity of care, Aguillard, Pierce, Benedict, and Burts (2005) investigated why only 13% of the children had the same primary caregiver throughout their time in the program. They interviewed the center directors to learn how the directors defined continuity of care, how they implemented it, and what barriers they thought obstructed its implementation. They found caregivers' preferences for working with a certain age group or *not* wanting to work with an age group and directors' perceptions of caregivers' inability to work with different age groups accounted for the majority of children's transitions from their primary caregivers.

Just as children differ from one another, teachers have expertise and preferences, as the next story illustrates.

I Just Like Them

I have taught different age groups and I can do it, but I have to push myself. But with my 2-year-olds, those older toddlers—I just like them. I love the continuity of being a toddler teacher and then seeing them go.

This teacher seems to nestle into the niche of her work with 2s. Teachers who work with the same age group repeatedly gain a sense of what to expect from children. The ensuing comfort can facilitate creative problem solving when the unexpected arises. Teachers can hone their curriculum ideas from previous years. Plus, children's interests, humor, and language use change as they develop, and, not surprisingly, adults may have preferences accordingly.

Inevitable Separations. People's lives change, and even when teachers, children, and families remain together, building close relationships for years, children eventually outgrow the program. Some adults avoid the raw emotions that close relationships with children evoke. Feelings of loss are inevitable when relationships end.

In the story that follows, a home visitor became close to a family through continuity with both parent and child. She ended the relationship when her life changed, and when she had the opportunity to reunite with them, she saw the ramifications of the break.

Changed Relationship

When I met with a family for the first time, they were welcoming. Their 12-month-old was open, not shy, and I started visiting them every week. The more we saw each other, the more our relationship grew. The mom told me about her life, about her other children, her hopes, her dreams. Our relationship was stable. I saw them every Tuesday at 9:00 a.m. Now the child is turning 2. She said "hi" when I arrived and "bye" when I left. Not all children do. It was a nice feeling to be part of her life.

In January, I left for nearly 6 months to pursue other interests. I've recently returned and was lucky to get that family on my caseload again. On my first return visit, though, I noticed it was not the same bond. Something was a little unstable. It felt new again. They were still loving and welcoming, but I felt like we had to get to know each other again. The child clearly remembered me, but she stayed closer to mom.

Now I've seen them four times. I'm still working to get to the place where we were before. After the third visit or so, the child warmed up. But I feel the mom is not as open as she was before. They are going on vacation for 2 months. I'm wondering how it will be when they get back.

In this story, the child was more receptive than her mom to picking up the thread of the previous relationship. Perhaps adults' past experiences make them cautious about renewing trust if continuity is interrupted. Or maybe the child in this story has a more adaptable temperament than that of her mother. Whatever the reason, some adults who work with children and families shy away from intense relationships.

COMPLICATIONS AND COMPLEXITIES

As you have read, continuity of care and children's continuity of experience is a complex matter. Structures can frame continuity of care but do not ensure relationships. Relationships can evolve without those structures in a climate in which adults are fully present. When teachers attend to the details of the child's day, know children well and recognize their agency, and work with families and colleagues to support relationships with children, children and adults can reap the benefits of close and caring relationships.

Complicating the issue, continuity is not what programs strive for in every instance, and discontinuity is not always undesirable. Discontinuity is a necessary element for growth. It is also unavoidable. Tronick (2007) contends that no mother can be responsive to her child all the time. In fact, ruptures in responsive care give children the chance to participate in regaining those moments of being in sync. Perhaps the same is true for relationships in care settings. Children will never have perfect caregivers, but they deserve people who are available to get back in sync with them. Then continuity in whatever form benefits children and adults alike.

CHAPTER 3

Continuity Between Home and School
What They Prefer

Consistent Communication

In our pre-K room, we still use the primary caregiving model. The primary teacher is the one who has consistent communication with a child's family. She's the one who writes the daily notes and knows the child best. The primary focus shifts, because the children are interested in relationships with each other and with all the teachers, but the family members still depend on the primary teacher for continuity of classroom experience and communication.

These 3-year-olds' social world has expanded from what it was when they were infants, and they no longer need primary caregivers—but their families still do. Families seek the teacher who knows their child. The personal connection becomes the conduit for continuity.

In this chapter, we turn from a focus on children's experiences and share stories that center on families and continuity between home and school. We use the terms *parent* and *family* to mean any adults who are responsible for the well-being of a child or children. This includes birth and adoptive parents, grandparents, foster care providers, and other such kin.

We listened as teachers and parents explored their expectations of each other. Sometimes we heard conflicting views about their respective roles. Their stories helped us to examine what home-school continuity looks like and how teachers and families might desire it and resist it and sometimes do both at the same time.

CREATING CONTINUITY BETWEEN HOME AND SCHOOL

Home-to-school continuity occurs when there are connections between home, school, and community that enable families and children to move from setting to setting with ease (Regional Educational Laboratories' Early Childhood Collaboration Network, 1995). When children move into an unfamiliar environment, they and their families form new relationships, with new roles and responsibilities. Providing children and families with continuity smoothes the many transitions that occur as children move from home to new and unfamiliar settings such as child care and elementary school.

What Can Continuity Look Like?

When parents and educators collaborate with one another, home-to-school continuity supports children's learning and development across contexts. Bronfenbrenner (1986) posited a model that locates the child in the center of concentric circles that represent the many and varied contexts of a child's life. He suggested that when children move from one setting to another such as from home to school, they experience either growth or alienation. And as young children move between settings so do their parents. They, too, may experience the unfamiliar as an opportunity to grow or may feel a sense of loss or separation. Each family, like each child, responds uniquely to new settings. For example, one parent may wish to stay in the classroom the entire 1st week. Another family may believe it is the children's job to learn how to handle the 1st day on their own. This parent might stand in the classroom doorway, wave to alert the teacher, kiss the child good-bye, and then leave. With these two perspectives and all the beliefs and resulting behaviors in between, families have varied reactions as they and their children experience movement between home and school.

According to Bronfenbrenner (1986) there are two factors that might assist young children, and probably parents, as they move between home and school: (1) the success with which the two settings relate to each other or are similar and (2) the extent to which the school or child care center is open to understanding the child and family's background and experiences. In the following section we look at the first concept to see how settings that feel similar to one another may facilitate congruence between home and school.

Early childhood education programs and parents can achieve continuity between home and school in a variety of ways. Parents seek out-of-home settings that seem similar to their values. Teachers, in turn, make provisions for new families to ease moving to an unfamiliar setting. Finally, parents and teachers collaborate, recognizing and acting upon their shared interest in and responsibility for the children.

Searching for Sameness. In the next story a parent talks about what she seeks in an educational setting for her child.

Finding a School That Fits

I looked hard to find a school for my daughter that reflects the values that I have, a school that would treat her as a whole kid. I had to do it for elementary school and then high school. I was looking for the same nurturing environment that we have at home. As you are growing, the themes that are strong stay with you.

This parent suggests that the messages a child receives within and outside the home and the values behind those messages influence a child's development and are therefore important to the parent. According to this parent, home-to-school continuity exists when the philosophy of a school, program, or teacher aligns with that of the parents.

The National Association for the Education of Young Children (NAEYC, 2009) advises parents, when they are looking for child care, to find a setting that shares similar beliefs about elements of care. In recommendations for choosing a toddler program, for example, NAEYC suggests that families look for a teacher whose views on discipline, weaning, and toileting are compatible with their own. According to NAEYC, the continuity between home and out-of-home settings will help toddlers learn positive behaviors. At the same time, these hoped-for similarities between home and school will reduce the discontinuity for the child.

Educators and families learn from each other and develop mutual understandings to facilitate children's educational experience (Rogoff, 1994). Both engage in listening with sensitivity toward the goal of understanding the perspective of the other (Gauvain, 2001). When parents and teachers understand each other's roles and expectations, they may discover they share values and common understandings about education and caregiving. They can begin to act in coordination with one another. Göncü, Abel, and Boshans (2010) describe this joint understanding of the world as *intersubjectivity*. Teachers and parents achieve intersubjectivity through a shared focus of attention on the child. In time, as parents and teachers communicate their beliefs, they build shared purpose and responsibility for educating and caring for a child.

The parent in the story "Finding a School That Fits" was fortunate. She could look for a school that was a good philosophical fit with her family. Yet not all parents can find a setting where they sense a connection or experience common understandings and intersubjectivity. Parents might not know that this is a possibility or may not have the resources to seek continuity through sameness.

Accommodation. In some cases, the family and the school share values and perspectives or come to share them. In other situations, one party accommodates the other or they resolve the situation in another way. The values embedded in a program may be quite different from the family's values. Parents adjust to the new educational setting, while teachers may accommodate to seek agreement and enhance the perception of a good fit. Other possibilities exist as well.

In the next story we meet a teacher who seeks common understandings with families—perhaps understanding their perspectives, but hoping most of all that they will come to see and adopt hers.

I Have to Teach Them

The families, I have to teach them. I invite them to come and see us and how we teach. For example, I made a big book with everything in English and Spanish that introduces the teachers in our room and talks about our curriculum, how we teach with simple activities. Most of the book is photos of the children at school with captions about what they are learning. It shows what's going on in the classrooms. Every family takes the book home for a week and returns it with a note about how they felt looking at the book. A family who complained that their child throws toys at home now does some things with the child at home instead of just watching TV.

Working with parents is not easy. Parents have different cultures and religions. A child who wouldn't eat vegetables at home ate them with me. I suggested, "You can try it at home." But some parents say, "No. My child only eats rice and beans." We talk about sleeping, toys, why we read to the children, why we go outside. Sometimes parents don't like it when children explore with sand and water. I explain everything.

This bilingual teacher makes an effort to establish and maintain a relationship with her families. She communicates her day-to-day practices in the classroom through photos in a book she created in the languages of the families served. She explains what she is doing and why she is doing it. This practice includes families and reflects her understanding that communication with families contributes to the development of the children in her care. The personal notes parents add when they return the book indicate the parents' pleasure in seeing what the children do when the parents are not present.

At the same time, though, this teacher admits that working with parents is not easy for her. She seems to want to teach the parents to understand and embrace her philosophy of education, or in her words, "how we teach" children. And it is not just classroom practices that this educator wants parents to understand and perhaps accept. In addition, she wishes the families used similar approaches with the children at home. We hear this sentiment when she talks about the child who ate vegetables with her but whose parent said the child eats only rice and beans at home.

The teacher hopes the parents will learn from her and from the way she and the children do things at school. According to Gonzalez-Mena (2005), this is one of the five types of accommodations in which teachers and families engage either explicitly or implicitly. The possible accommodations or resolutions to conflict are the following:

- Parent education
- Teacher education
- Compromise through negotiation
- Ongoing management of unresolved conflict
- Mutual education

In the previous scenario the teacher is engaging in *parent education*. She wants the families to learn about school from her. She informs the parents about classroom practices and her beliefs about child development.

The next type of accommodation is *teacher education*. In this case, a teacher learns from the parent to understand how the family does things. The teacher or program then changes to meet the family's wishes. This occurs, for example, when a toddler teacher asks family members how their child might best be soothed to sleep. Here is another example of a teacher learning from a parent:

Compórtate Bien

Every morning when Jorge's mother dropped him off, she said, "Compórtate bien" [Behave yourself] and gave him a little push. Once when I said to her, "Jorge always behaves well," she gave me a strange look. I realized after some reflection and reading that her job was to make sure her son behaved, reflecting well on the family and setting him up for school success. My job was to teach him, not to interfere with her role.

Some families feel that home and school are two separate entities, no matter the age of the child. As one parent said, "I get my kids dressed and fed in the morning and get them to school on time. Your job is to teach them." Although she expressed that feeling nonverbally, Jorge's mother seemed to agree. Her son's teacher learned from her about another way of seeing their roles.

The next point concerning compromise or resolution is *compromise through negotiation*. This happens as the parent and teacher talk and come to some agreement that is not what either one started with but involves meeting each other halfway. The following is an illustrative story.

"Stop Active Listening Me"

I could see that it was frustrating—three times Michael left his wet bathing suit and towel in the lockers at the Y, and his dad came charging in to retrieve them. His dad told me how mad he was, and I nodded and repeated what he was saying. He finally said, "Stop active listening me and do something about it!" His outburst overwhelmed me, and I told him I would be sure that his son had his suit in his backpack before leaving the Y, but I asked if the dad could pin a note to his son's backpack to remind him of his responsibility to bring home his belongings. The dad admitted begrudgingly, "I guess he is old enough to remember his stuff."

This 5-year-old's father and teacher had their own expectations—the parent wanted the teacher to be responsible for swimming gear, whereas the teacher wanted the child to learn responsibility through the consequences of the child's actions. They made a deal that worked for them both.

Sometimes, instead of coming to a resolution, parent and teacher or parent and director never reach any kind of agreement. Bad feelings may underlie the relationship on one or both parts. Here is a story from a teacher that illustrates what Gonzalez-Mena calls the *ongoing management of unresolved conflict*.

Raising His Son to Survive

There was a young boy, 1½ to 2 when he started; he would fix his face to look stern and move his shoulders and fingers to flash gang signs in front of the mirror—his face was so intense, very aggressive. He took on a gang persona. His play was a direct reflection of what he saw at home. He wanted to be like his dad. He missed his dad.

The director thought it was atrocious and said, "We need to talk to mom, she's raising her son to be a gang banger." In the director's mind it was an embarrassment. She called a meeting with the parent to talk about the child's play. The parent was ashamed. The director was so disrespectful to the mom. She demanded the mom tell the father to stop playing with the child that way. The father drove 85 miles to the school, so angry that he cursed from the time he walked in until he walked back out the door. He's raising his son to survive. The mother got her ass beat, because she told on the father. . . . The child's play was actually soothing him.

While the unresolved conflict is between the director and family members, the teacher, as an observer of the conflict, and the child, too, live with it. In the end, neither parents nor director changed their position.

The last point, *mutual education,* refers to when an educator and parent learn from each other, creating a "third space" (Barrera & Corso, 2003). Unlike in compromise, both parties come up with something that is different from both of their original ideas but is acceptable to all. In nurturing a third space, teachers and parents accept that there are multiple realities and then engage in dialogue instead of arguing or even negotiating. It involves a willingness to allow different points of view, making way for new and deeper understandings of how things could be. The following story is an example of third space but shows, too, how it may not achieve an ideal.

Punching

I was working with teen parents at the residence where they lived with their children. One mom was really rough with her kids both verbally and physically. I reminded her of my mandated reporter status and that I expected her not to hit or grab her children while we were in session together. She said, "This is how I'm raising my kids. They're my kids." We talked a lot. In our conversations, it became clear that she wasn't going to agree with my way of disciplining children, and I wasn't going to agree with hers. Neither of us could compromise.

As time went on, we continued talking and built a relationship, and we started to understand each other. She started using language that I used with the children. I started to understand her sense of humor and noticed her strengths as a mother. She chose to do what she called "time-outs" for her 2-year-old instead of hitting him. She'd say to him, "You know I'm not going to punch you, because she's here" (meaning me), "but you better just sit over there and think about this for a while." She watched me carefully to see if I was going to interfere with her disciplining. Sometimes she'd scream at her kids that she was going to punch them, and I could see from their faces that they could tell if she was serious or not.

One time she was trying to get her 9-month-old to show me how he could stand and walk, but he kept sitting down. She would lift him up, he'd plop down, and she'd threaten to punch him, but you could see that she was teasing and that he wasn't scared. They were playing a game and both accepted and understood the rules. He seemed to understand that she wasn't going to hurt him.

In the course of our relationship with each other, this mom invented new ways of disciplining her children, and I learned about the meanings behind her choices and her behaviors. This became really clear to me when I showed a video clip of the mom and her 2-year-old to a class I was taking. My classmates commented on the rough way she spoke to the children. It bothered them, but I knew it was just her style. I had come to understand more about her and the way she parented her children.

Both teacher and parent learned from each other and about each other. They found some continuity in a third space that was neither all one of theirs nor all the other's and lived with the remaining discontinuity. Families do not change just because teachers want them to, but at the same time, teachers cannot compromise professional beliefs and ethical values. In this story, the teacher and parent did not make a deal or compromise. They found a third space together.

Handling conflicts and making accommodations with families may be one of the hardest tasks of a teacher. Not only do educators need to understand the parent's perspective; they also must identify the need for an accommodation, reflect on how to make it happen, and then manage the emotions that arise. In addition, teachers might model for parents how to work through conflicts and ways to express difficult feelings (Keyser, 2006).

Accommodation is an aspect of building any effective relationship. Other components are trust, commitment, and predictability. In a sense, home-to-school connection is based on the creation of relationship continuity between families and programs. Teachers create relationship continuity when they work to build partnerships with families.

Building Bridges for Partnership

Parents are the main decisionmakers concerning their child's care and education. Purposeful home-to-school interactions, planned by the teacher, create the foundation for partnerships between educators and families. In these partnerships, families and teachers share information such as goals, engage in ongoing communication, and acknowledge the strengths both bring to the child's development and learning (Rouse, 2012). In theory, these partnerships set the context for relationship continuity and consistency as children move from home to child care and education settings and back home.

One way to ensure that home and school settings relate to each other is to design classroom structures and program policies that facilitate home-to-school continuity. In the next section we listen to teachers as they discuss strategies to make out-of-home child care or formal school-ing a comfortable transition for families, perhaps with the recognition that the two settings can be quite different from one another.

Making Provisions for New Children and Families. Not only must children adjust to new settings and expectations; so must parents. In the next story, we hear how a teacher plans for continuity for the infants, toddlers, and families in her care.

She Won't Miss Me

I worked at a child care program for infants and toddlers whose parents were studying to take the GED exam and prepare for jobs. My first consideration was bringing both the child and parent into the center and encouraging both to feel comfortable in this environment that was different from the home environment. I wanted them both to get used to it. I especially wanted the child to feel comfortable at the center before the parent went off to class. We wanted to set up a separation period so that the children would be feeling that they got to know us before they were left with us. This idea of a separation process was foreign to some of the parents and to their employment counselors who didn't want the parents to miss any classes. As people outside the field of early childhood, they hadn't heard or discussed the theory and maybe didn't see it as important or their ideas were different or they just didn't want to be bothered. We stuck to our guns to make it an easier transition for the children. It's worth it for the parents to be exposed to this idea. It was a new concept to some parents that their child might miss them or that the shock a very young child might feel upon being separated from someone they were attached to could be minimized. Parents would say, "Oh, she won't miss me." They had the feeling that the child could adapt.

This educator saw a difference between her views of children starting a program and the parents' perceptions of their children's experience. She planned a process through which parents and children became comfort-able in the new setting. Gradually introducing the child to the classroom helps children make the transition to a new group setting, whether they have been at home or at a different school. Although the purpose of a gradual transition is for children to become comfortable in a new set-ting, it can help families as well. Families may need time and support to adjust to the out-of-home setting. The educator in the story "She Won't Miss Me" believes a slow and supported transition from home to school is worthwhile. She understands that this transition process is not just for children, but also for parents. She continues:

The separation process gives parents a chance to get to know the environment also and can establish some continuity between what a child already knows and what they're coming into. The children could see, too, that their parent was putting a stamp of approval on this program and that it was okay for them to be there.

Their parents' "stamp of approval" along with children's secure feelings in the new setting ease the transition from home to school.

Families and children need time to learn to manage the new and unfamiliar systems of child care centers, schools, and agencies that work with children and families. Children intuit their parents' feelings about the setting and feel more or less secure there as a result.

In the next story we hear from an education coordinator who sought to build a secure relationship with a parent.

Sign the Form

A parent was in her 2nd year at our Head Start program and was still disconnected from everybody. We realize that children need consistency and to be able to depend on us and trust us. The same is true for the parents, but this parent lashed out at us, especially if we asked her to do anything, for example, come to a meeting. She was always disgruntled. We tried to give her child whatever he needed to grow academically and socially, yet the mom resisted us. "Why do I have to fill out this form?"; and she would walk away without completing it.

I believe continuity is important for scaffolding and for the consistency that people can trust. I realized that this parent wanted what her children were getting, that same nurturing and consistency that she had never gotten. She has lots of reasons for being the way she is. She's really pretty, but her face is always in a scowl. She scared other parents and the rest of the staff.

So I treated her the way I treated her son. I went to her, and I put my hand on her shoulder. I explained why she had to fill out the form for her son's eye exam. This mom is in school and is a conscientious student. One day after the incident with the eye exam, she was falling apart. She cried for 2 hours, because the assistant on her son's bus had called her irresponsible. I tried to help her understand that she's not irresponsible. I said, "You are strong and doing amazing things for your children." I helped her figure out what to say to the bus assistant. Now she is warmer. We have a relationship.

Upon entering a new setting, for instance, a preschool, parents such as this mother may not appear to want a relationship with their child's teacher. Parents can worry that teachers will judge their parenting. Some families do not think that it will be possible to form a relationship with a teacher. It simply is not something they saw their parents do when they went to school, so they do not attempt an affiliation with their child's teacher. In this story the Head Start education coordinator decided to initiate the relationship, even when the parent was "disconnected."

Barriers to Bridge Building. Families may seem disconnected from their children's classroom or school for many reasons. Barriers may be raised when parents (1) fear that they are not educated enough to engage, (2) have insufficient information on home and school relationship possibilities, (3) live with inflexible or stressful work schedules and situations, (4) lack confidence, (5) have different expectations of the role of schools and parents, or (6) experience discomfort based on their own schooling.

Despite barriers that confronted the parent, the education coordinator in the story "Sign the Form" initiated a relationship. This can be tough for educators because they, too, face barriers to effective relationships with families (Caplan, 2000). Teachers feel they do not have the time to develop relationships with families or that the workplace focuses on children and not on the families. Some teachers may fear criticism from parents and thus avoid them. Or perhaps in her childhood, an educator's parents did not participate in any school event, and forming parent–teacher relationships is awkward and unfamiliar territory.

If home-to-school continuity is dependent upon connections between families and teachers, not just between children and teachers, an educator must navigate the possible barriers that make relationship building a challenge. Teachers establish relationships through self-reflection; effort; interest; and appreciation of children and their families, even those that they find challenging.

Cheatham and Jimenez-Silva (2012) found three factors for teachers to consider when building true partnerships with families: culture, language, and power. Different cultures view the power in teacher and parental roles differently and have a range of interaction styles, behavioral expectations, and educational goals. Of course, communication and collaboration are difficult if teachers and families speak different languages. And early educators must strive to share power with parents in order to develop partnerships. Next, we look at these intertwining factors more closely.

UNDERSTANDING DIFFERENCES

In the previous section we heard from teachers who hope that similarity between home and school will create continuity for children and their families. They aim for continuity, believing that continuity between home and school promotes growth rather than alienation. In the next section, we discuss another source of continuity that many believe assists with the movement between home and school: the extent to which the school and teacher are open to understanding the child and family's cultural background and experiences. In some situations, work with families fosters similarities between home and school. In others it embraces the differences.

The Intercontextual Nature of Relationships

Families and schools share the responsibility for nurturing children's development and learning. This is called the *intercontextual nature of relationships* between schools and families (Lightfoot, 1978). Both families and schools function in the context of the other. Families interact with teachers in the world of the school. Teachers work with children and families with the ever-present influence of the families' culture.

Multiple Contexts of Families and Children. In the next two stories we listen to preschool teachers, both of whom self-identify as Latina and work within the same border-community school. Both believe their role is to build connections between the families they serve and their school setting. Both want more continuity between home and school, but they approach that project differently.

Education at Home

A challenge I face is discontinuity between the school and home setting. Working with the children, I often see that their education is not supported at home. This is a challenge for me, because I need to ensure that their learning is meaningful and that home connections are made. I have numerous questions about how to help parents become more involved in their child's education. The children come to us and don't know how to act in that social setting, don't know what to do. I see how parents can help them; parents could read and talk to them. I see students who lack communication skills. Even those minor things we value in our setting, they don't have. During parent–teacher conferences I emphasize simple games and ways to communicate at home. At school, we are educating the parents as well as the children.

Similar to the educator who told us, "I have to teach them," in the story of that title, this teacher wishes she could educate the parents as well as the children. She believes that her students would benefit from parents engaging at home in educational activities such as playing simple games and reading aloud. The teacher wants the parents to help her reach the educational outcomes that will make their children successful in school. For example, she values rich reciprocal verbal exchanges between parent and child, believing that they will produce enhanced vocabulary development, which, in turn, will lead to strong reading skills (Hart & Risley, 1995). So the educator wishes the parents would read and talk to the children at home to enhance literacy skill development.

In the "Education at Home" story we hear from a teacher who wishes families would behave more like teachers. Yet this concept of home-school continuity is unrealistic, because many children come from homes where school-like activities will not occur. Parents may feel uncomfortable engaging in such activities with young children at home or they may not have the time or resources for them. As discussed earlier, some families believe that the school is responsible for teaching children, rather than the parents doing so. Other parents might view these educational activities as unimportant or inappropriate for young children.

At the same school a different teacher shared her story.

Pumpkin Glow

I work at a small preschool where we are trying to have collaboration with bicultural families, 98% of whom are Latino. We do home visits, have birthday celebrations, holidays, but we want parents there at school, not just on certain occasions. In the fall, we took the children to a pumpkin patch, and every child received a pumpkin to carve at home. Then we invited all the parents to a social event, the Pumpkin Glow. Educationally, we work in a low-income community, where parents leave education just to us. There's a barrier between us and the families. Families have other values that we don't take into consideration that we should. A lot of families are artistic; we saw that with the pumpkins they carved, and that made a connection between families and ourselves. You should have seen pumpkins people carved. They went above and beyond. The families—everybody knows each other. At our Pumpkin Glow they talked about their children and themselves. Now parents are asking for more events. It actually got out of hand. We weren't prepared for so many people. Families—with grandparents and neighbors—came in groups of 10.

Now we can plan for something similar and be prepared. We are asking for more resources from our district. We already have returning families and see the difference in our relationship with them from first child to second child. We have continuity with families over the years. We have built our relationships with the children's parents through social events, which is what they prefer. We are learning and teaching nonmainstream values that reflect the families in our program.

In both these stories the teachers remark that the parents leave their children's education to the teachers, but the teachers of these stories differ in their approaches to the families. Each of them says she values and wants what she does not think parents provide. The first teacher says she values communication skills. The second says she wants parents to come to school—not just "on certain occasions." Yet the second teacher has found a way to bring school and home together through a social event called the Pumpkin Glow where families "talked about their children and themselves." The teacher noticed that over the years this event has built "continuity with families" and there is a "difference in our relationship with [the families] from first child to second child."

Both teachers originally hoped to increase the similarity between home and school, but the first teacher wanted home to become more like school. The second teacher grew to understand the importance of respecting, building upon, and including families' interests and knowledge. She learned that "families have other values that we don't take into consideration that we should." Although in the community "everybody knows each other," neither teachers nor families seemed to consider the school a place for social connection. The Pumpkin Glow enabled families to see the school as an extension of their community and gave the teachers a way to connect with families. The teacher in the "Pumpkin Glow" story decided that for the families with whom she works, home-school continuity occurs through non-school-like activities where parent, teacher, and community relationships can develop.

Bronfenbrenner's ecology of human development concept provided a theoretical lens through which to understand the importance of home-to-school connections for the child. Vygotsky's (1978) sociocultural theory, which emphasizes the importance of social context and social interactions, offers a second theoretical lens. Social context includes the history, culture, and institutional contexts that shape development and children's view of the world. Vygotsky perceived children as active agents who learn to use cultural tools to master actions such as transitions. Children's social understandings and interactions provide a basis for new ways of engaging in different contexts (Rogoff, 2003). This theory explains how children, families, and educators change when they participate in relevant and meaningful new events. It also points out how the event changes over time as a result of their participation. Taken together, Bronfenbrenner's ecological theory and Vygotsky's sociocultural theory promote a view of development informed by the multiple contexts in which children and families develop and the interactions between these contexts or systems.

The teacher from the "Pumpkin Glow" story continues, "We are learning and teaching nonmainstream values that reflect the families in our program." What she means by "nonmainstream values," we think, are the essential knowledge and skills that families possess because they reside in a specific community with culturally and historically accumulated ways of being. These funds of knowledge (González, Moll, & Amanti, 2005) pertain to religion, work, and household management. Funds of knowledge include the material, scientific, and agricultural knowledge that resides with families and communities. The cultural knowledge and skill that the families possess, in, for example, their embrace of the arts, has a place in her vision of school alongside academic knowledge.

Teachers who are aware of and understand the funds of knowledge that families possess can capitalize on cultural diversity and minimize the discontinuity between home environments and the culture of school. When they encourage families to share their funds of knowledge and make such knowledge part of the educational setting, teachers are better positioned to enhance a child's learning.

Listening to Learn. The term *cultural continuity* describes an educator's ability to listen, understand, respect, and build upon the cultural and linguistic practices of the home. It also refers to the decisions programs make based on the multiple cultural contexts of the children served. Culture is the "ever-changing values, traditions, social and political relationships, and worldview created, shared, and transformed by a group of people bound together by a combination of factors that can include a common history, geographic location, language, social class, and religion" (Nieto & Bode, 2008, p. 171).

Culture is not just ethnicity or race; it includes a diversity of lifestyles, family structures, and ways of being in the world. In programs that are culturally congruent with children and their families, teachers understand that cultural beliefs, norms, and values guide behavior and expectations for themselves and the families and children with whom they work. They support each child's continued growth and development with efforts to understand children in their family contexts and have open and ongoing dialogue with families.

In this next story we hear from a teacher who is observing a child at play and making efforts to understand his play.

Ironing on the Floor

A little boy really liked to iron and would turn things into ironing. He would iron all day long. At first, we did not understand what he was doing. We thought maybe he needs to try something else. He would take random pieces of fabric, put them on the floor, and rub blocks over them. His parent said, "Well, he's ironing." We brought in an ironing board, but he still did it on the floor. We don't understand why he's ironing on the floor. His mother said, "He's never seen an ironing board. I iron on the floor."

This teacher observed the child closely, brought in props, and then turned to the parent to gain understandings of this child's representational play. She continued,

> We were trying to make connections and brought in the ironing board. We paid particular attention to how this kid put fabric on the floor, all his steps. Yet how we were expanding experiences might have confused a child and offended the family.

Listening for understanding is important for all teachers. Continuity is rooted in relationships in which teachers know and continue to learn about the children and families with whom they work. This includes what families and children bring to the classroom and how they go about their lives.

In the next story we hear from a child life specialist. Trained in child development and family systems, child life specialists work in hospitals and other health care settings to assist families and children to cope with illness and hospitalization. Here this specialist is volunteering internationally to work with children and families. The children are scheduled for surgery, and she works with them before and afterward.

She Knew Her Child Better

A mother in Amman told me her son was really scared and that she hadn't really told him anything [about the operation], nor did she want to tell him anything. So while he was playing with some Peace Corps volunteers, I showed her the photo book of what to expect in surgery. She looked through it carefully. I told her that we like to prepare children for what they're going to see and experience, so it won't be as scary. After she read the book, she called her son over, and she started going through the book with him.

Later, with an interpreter, I asked her what she had said to him. She told me that he was very interested in computers and TV, so she had shown him the photo of the operating room that has the heart monitor in it. And she told him that's what he was going to see. I had to really sit on my wish to tell him more and to trust that she knew her child better than I did. And he did fine.

To learn about the preferences of family members, teachers need to be close observers and good listeners. In this story the child life specialist also had to trust the mother's knowledge of her son rather than impose her own preconceived expectations onto the family. As a child life specialist she was accustomed to preparing children for what was to come, yet she was able to follow this mother's approach to her child's surgery.

Whose Culture Do We Include?

Continuity between the child's experiences in the home and in the early childhood program is a key feature of culturally responsive education (Neuman & Roskos, 1994). A teachers' knowledge of a child's home, family configuration, and cultural community facilitates the transition from home to school. In the next story, a staff development specialist described how a director resisted supporting cultural continuity for one form of family diversity.

An Open and Heated Discussion

Last week we had a meeting with the directors from our five early childhood sites and the two of us who are staff development specialists. We talked to the teachers about the upcoming Diversity Conference. It will be open to teachers and we invited directors to encourage teachers to propose workshops to present.

We define diversity broadly and talked about how, although some children at our centers have gay or lesbian parents, those families are not represented in the classrooms. This launched a 30-minute discussion that was both open and heated. One center director in particular said, "Why do we have to talk about it?" She defended her position with "We don't have to put it in their faces. They already know about their families." She saw no need for books, images, or conversations with children and felt very strongly about this.

The two of us who are the staff development specialists were vocal, but the other four directors were absolutely quiet. We tried to push that director to think about why she supports other languages and represents a variety of religious observances at holiday times. She shows disabilities, although there are no children in wheelchairs at her center. Why doesn't this type of diversity count? The director answered, "No, but I'm saying . . . the children are too young."

I've seen people argue in ways that are more clearly homophobic. This director couched her position in child development and the needs of the larger group, claiming that representation of gay- and lesbian-headed families at her center would be "confusing to the children." She said that if people are not in the building, it's too abstract for children. I asked her, "But what about children who never see or hear their family represented?" She answered, "We say everybody's different, and everybody's comfortable with their own family."

This staff developer expressed concern that children and parents from same-sex families need to be explicitly welcomed into the preschool setting to be members of that school community. Research indicates that same-sex parents may feel ignored, excluded, and mistreated by schools (Kosciw, Greytak, Diaz, & Bartkiewicz, 2008). Families report that these feelings emerge because of subtle forms of exclusion such as lack of acknowledgment (Adams & Persinger, 2013). One example is the admission forms that ask for the name of one mother and one father. LGBT (lesbian, gay, bisexual, transgender) parents, grandparents, adoptive parents, foster parents, single parents, or step-parents may feel excluded as well.

Inclusive atmospheres where all families feel welcomed are a beginning step toward home-school continuity. Parents can more easily trust a program that recognizes them as a family and that they can count on to be emotionally safe for their child. The National Association of School Psychologists (Adams & Persinger, 2013) recommends strategies for working with LGBT parents that can apply to all families:

- Encourage teachers to recognize their biases and misconceptions and how these ideas are contrary to making home-to-school connections.
- Develop policies that state clearly that the program will not permit biased language and actions from teachers and administrators.
- Identify biased language in program literature and forms and rewrite it to be inclusive.
- Directly ask families how they wish teachers and administrators to address them.
- Invite all families to participate in classroom and school events; one-to-one, face-to-face invitations work best.
- Create a family bulletin board at the entrance of the school with posters and other materials from organizations representing the

diversity of the community and invite families to connect with the larger community.

The "open and heated" discussion in the previous story illustrates discontinuity, because the director does not believe that preschools should openly acknowledge gay and lesbian families. When she refuses to make their family structures visible, she isolates those families from the school, and that isolation constitutes a discontinuity between home and school for those families. She seems to dismiss home-to-school continuity as unnecessary in this case.

In this story we also hear the director's belief that children are too young to understand that some children have same-sex parents. She defended her position using a selective understanding of child development. When she claimed that young children cannot comprehend LGBT families, because the notion is too confusing and abstract for them, she was not giving children credit for what they can grasp. In fact, many of the children at her school know about the families with whom they interact. In particular, the children living in these families obviously know they have two moms or two dads. Thus, this story illustrates two distinct yet connected discontinuities: the belief that children are too young to comprehend what is in the everyday of their lives and that only certain types of families warrant acknowledgment at school.

NAVIGATING DISCONTINUITIES

When school and home are somewhat similar and presumably well matched, children and families can experience a feeling of continuity. In addition, teachers and families who attempt to understand each other across differences can also achieve continuity. For some children and families, however, the home-school connection involves discontinuity of relationships, curriculum, resources, and support (Dockett & Perry, 2007; Rimm-Kaufman & Pianta, 2000). Teachers and parents say that continuity between home and school requires them to navigate transitions and new relationships on an ongoing basis. Many of our stories suggest that families and teachers recognize that they cannot avoid discontinuity and need to embrace it. As Ghaye and Pascal (1988) suggest, it may be more important to deal directly with discontinuity than attempt to maintain continuity.

Preparing for Discontinuity

Many resources can guide educators in establishing home-to-school connections. This next section is a concise list modified from the work of Keyser (2006).

For Families. To support families through times of discontinuity, familiarize families and children with the culture of the school, share expectations from home and school, and help children and families feel ownership of the school. Briefly, programs and teachers assist families when they do the following:

- Make the family's first contact with the school welcoming and informative.
- Offer formal and informal orientation/enrollment activities that convey the core value that families are partners in decisionmaking. These include family handbooks, orienting families to both the people and the program, allowing time to be in the classroom, creating a family-meeting space, and providing language support.
- Directly acknowledge and listen for families' feelings about the transition from home to school and share resources with the families.
- Engage in community and home visits to let the family know their context is important to you.

For Teachers. Plan for school-to-home and home-to-school communication through these strategies:

- Create opportunities for daily communication such as check-ins with families if they come to the classroom; brief individual notes; and whole-group announcements regarding the day's activities, reminders, and requests.
- Produce interactive family journals created by both the families and teachers to share information and decisionmaking. This two-way communication tool can include the teacher's anecdotal notes and photos, and families can write back or just enjoy hearing about the child's days.
- Engage in worthwhile sharing times such as face-to-face meetings/conferences and phone calls.
- Facilitate specific parent engagement opportunities in and outside the classroom, at home, and in the community.
- Know your own values and goals and be an effective cross-cultural communicator.

Expecting the Unexpected

Even with preparation, families may approach home-to-school transitions and connections in ways that teachers do not expect. For example, the parent of a 14-month-old child told us, "I'm just tired of being bombarded with the daily poo report. Why don't they tell me what my daughter has done today?" Although it is common practice for infant and toddler teachers to give parents an update on children's physical care and responses during the day, this parent was frustrated and wanted to know more about her daughter's day than whether or not she had a bowel movement.

As in all relationships, continuity in home-to-school interactions requires a lot of work and may not always be possible. Parents and teachers have unspoken expectations, assumptions, and as discussed earlier, diverse childrearing beliefs and values. Building partnerships is the goal, yet teachers need to navigate the inevitable discontinuities of relationships. In the next section we hear stories of discontinuity that may be familiar to teachers.

What Rules Apply? Some families consider spanking an effective form of child discipline. Some early childhood teachers may spank their sons and daughters, too. However most early childhood programs have a policy of no physical discipline and use practices of child guidance rather than punishment. These practices, rooted in developmental psychology, are to guide children's behavior, slowly moving toward child self-regulation through adult support rather than punishment. In the next story we hear from a teacher who believes in continuity between home and school but who struggles with one form of incongruity—discipline.

Hard for Kids

I worked with children whose families used physical discipline. The children weren't used to verbal means of discipline. I think that was a big difficulty for them at the center. They came in to this early childhood setup, and we wanted more continuity between home and school. Still, we wouldn't use the physical means for disciplining children, and it is confusing for them. When the children misbehaved, it was hard for them to understand that we may talk or not allow them to use an activity—that whole piece is hard for kids.

The teacher realizes that children have to juggle two approaches when home and school respond differently to "misbehavior." The teachers do not believe that spanking children will teach them to self-regulate. The parents do not think talking through an issue with a young child will work, nor is it how they were raised. Meanwhile, programs are beholden to licensing regulations that do not allow physical discipline. According to Baumrind (1991), the differing approaches or responses to child behavior are rooted in four dimensions. The first is nurturance, the amount and type of care and concern adults express to children. The second is expectations, the standards adults set for children's behavior. Next is communication, the amount and type of information and instruction adults offer children about how to behave. And the final element is control, the amount and type of ways adults enforce children's compliance with their expectations.

When the adults at home and school differ in the emphasis they place on each of these dimensions, the child may need time to adjust to the new code of conduct and resulting consequences in the classroom. And this new code, as deemed appropriate by the social norms and values of the teacher and program, is one powerful form of discontinuity for children and their families.

Making Room for Vulnerability. While children are meeting new teachers and accommodating a different environment with new rules, families are adjusting too. Kreider (2002) interviewed parents as their child transitioned from preschool or home to kindergarten. The parents expressed happiness because their children were excited about starting kindergarten. The parents perceived the new setting as an opportunity to make friends and learn. They also voiced sadness related to the child's "leaving the nest" and the change in their own identity at this new phase of childhood. Last, the parents worried. They worried about their child's vulnerabilities.

Parents are vulnerable as well. To imagine how they might feel, WestEd's "Valuable Possession" exercise challenges educators to think of a most prized possession. Imagine a stranger taking it away and saying, "I'll take care of your valuable possession every day. I'll take good care of it and might even change it a little. You can pick it up at the end of each day, but you'll need to bring it back to me the next morning." This exercise simulates some parents' daily experience.

Even though many parents can choose their child's early education program, they experience a sense of loss and a perceived lack of control. Even the best environment can produce worries. A mother told us a story of one such situation.

Falling Asleep

When our son was 2½, my partner was doing the long hours of her residency quite far from where we lived. I worked at a university about an hour of tedious city driving from home, and our son attended the excellent child care center there. When I taught in the evenings, he could stay at the center until I picked him up. As we drove home, he pointed out cars and trucks until about halfway through the ride, when he fell asleep. Then there I was, parking the car with a dog to walk and a sleeping child to wake up or carry—in cold, snow, or rain. What was wrong with this picture? I had some of the best child care in the country, and it wasn't working for me.

Sometimes even the best care environments do not work for families. Perhaps part of home-to-school continuity is creating ways to support families' daily lives. Another parent told us a story about a less stressful transition.

The Fruit Bowl

When Antonio was in child care all day I would pick him up around 5:30. We were both tired and hungry and still had a bit of a drive home. I remember one day I went to the cubbies to pick up Antonio's belongings and sign him out. There, next to the clipboard, was a big bowl of fruit. A note said "for the ride home." It was perfect! After that day, Antonio would come in from the playground a little quicker. He would then take his time and choose a snack for the ride home—usually just leftovers from lunch, such as fruit or crackers—from the bowl. But it made leaving preschool and going home easier. It became a ritual for us.

Here was a new form of home-to-school, or rather school-to-home, continuity that the child care teacher offered the families at the end of the day. Imagine other ways in which an educator could assist families with daily transitions to promote continuity in the morning or evening.

Erasing the Discontinuity/Continuity Binary

Teachers and programs are proactive with efforts to build home-to-school continuity. Yet discontinuity and continuity are not either/or choices. Instead of separating these concepts into opposites it might be more fruitful to view them as reciprocal. The movement between home and school and school to home is an ongoing give-and-take among the families; teachers; program policies and administrators; and the multiple contexts of child care, schooling, and communities.

These stories ask us to look at home-to-school continuity from the perspective of families along with that of the school. When the focus is on the home, we look at ways in which culture and communities perceive and perhaps prepare for home-to-school continuity. Baker, Kessler-Sklar, Piotrkowski, and Parker (1999) discovered that educators often have limited knowledge of the supports parents put into place to help their child succeed in school. Teachers who are busy creating well-meaning home-school projects, but who do not recognize and learn from the families themselves, can do more harm than good, as Valdez (1996) found in her study of Mexican immigrants. This is consistent with Mapp's (2003) findings that administrative or school-based family initiatives such as newsletters and open houses are important to parents, but the establishment of relationships is particularly salient.

Teachers navigate the landscape of relationships as they take an inquisitive stance and interrupt their own expectations (Delpit, 1988). They start with each family's home as a point of reference, and they listen and learn to understand and prepare a welcoming and engaging environment. Educators anticipate that home-to-school continuity is created through the willingness to build respectful relationships.

CHAPTER 4

Continuity in Systems
Figuring It All Out

Evolving Roles

As the director of a center for 3- to 5-year-olds, my role has evolved. We went from being babysitters to planning activities based on children's developmental needs. Our roles continue to change into those of child care advocates, teachers, curriculum specialists, nurses, and custodians. We are investing in mental health and counseling, too. Our families have higher risks, and we focus on the whole family.

This director tells how her center has come to serve families better. It evolved from a single "babysitting" service into an ecological system of support that connects to medical, psychological, and other resources. The center became part of a larger set of systems when it began to offer more to children and families. The center changed, not because of a mandate but because these systems made sense based on what the center staff knew about children's families. When the director described the path from babysitters to child advocates, she also seemed to be describing her center's recent membership in a larger early childhood community—in a system. Throughout this chapter, you will hear stories about children's and families' transitions as they move through existing systems. You will also read about changes that administrators and policy makers effect in their efforts to create new systems.

We begin by defining what early childhood systems are and examining how they can create continuity and discontinuity for children, families, and teachers. We also look at why, despite the best intentions and efforts of early childhood decisionmakers, continuity within and between systems is elusive and, perhaps, problematic.

UNDERSTANDING SYSTEMS

A system is a grouping of interconnected elements, an assemblage of interrelated parts that, together, create a more complex and continuous whole. A well-functioning system provided support to one mother and her child as they made the transition from preschool to kindergarten. However, a subsequent transition within that educational system revealed "cracks" through which her child could fall.

Falling Through the Cracks

I think everybody does a good job working with a young child who has a disability. The transition team, the school's IEP [individualized education plan] team, the new kindergarten teacher and parents, and the disability coordinator all met together when my child moved from private preschool to kindergarten. We did it well.

But when I moved my child from one public school to another—in the same district—when he was in 2nd grade, it did not go well. If I hadn't been a vocal parent, my child would have fallen through the cracks. We had an IEP meeting at the new school and the disability coordinator said, "We have no idea what happened to all the paperwork." They had no information about my son. It had been 60 days, and I wanted to know where we were with my son's evaluation as required by signed contract. Yet nothing had been done.

This story illustrates both successful and unsuccessful transitions between systems and settings. The first transition in this parent's story involved the early childhood system (private child care), elementary education system (kindergarten teacher), the family system, and the health and social services system (the disability coordinator). That transition was successful. The second transition was difficult. Any transition between systems or between settings within a system creates an opportunity for continuity and discontinuity. The outcome of that opportunity depends, as you have read in previous chapters, on the actions of the individuals who are part of those systems.

People who write about early childhood systems think about the systems in different ways. The story that opens this chapter describes an early childhood system that links social, economic, and physical services (see also Center for Law and Social Policy, 2011). Picture a family that is new to the United States. A comprehensive early childhood program might offer them assistance with housing, English classes for the adults, and access to medical services. Such a system can provide families and children with a coherent and supportive experience.

Another way to conceptualize early childhood systems (e.g., Kagan & Kauerz, 2012) is as linked educational institutions that can operate separately, as in early childhood programs and elementary schools. Connecting the two in a single system could create a more continuous experience for children and families. Kindergarten teachers, for example, could receive developmental information from their children's Head Start and begin the school year with baseline data.

In both these approaches to early childhood systems, components of the system work together. They support children's growth, development, and learning. That implicit shared mission to support the education and well-being of children holds the elements of each system together.

Why Have an Early Childhood System?

Early childhood systems can serve different purposes. The goal behind any system determines the nature of the system itself. What follows are two examples of systems that have different aims, based on different underlying premises.

Ecologically Based Systems. Commitment to children's well-being is one goal for building early childhood systems (Bruner, 2012). Those who subscribe to this purpose recognize that children grow and families live and work within an interconnected ecological system (Bronfenbrenner, 1979).

When one applies Bronfenbrenner's ecological systems theory to system building in early childhood, one takes a holistic look at the child in context. Through this theoretical lens, a well-organized and coordinated system of early childhood can result in opportunities for children to learn and grow in linked early childhood settings. Concomitantly, a network of linked agencies and service providers that support the health and welfare of their families would further contribute to positive early learning outcomes.

Systems for Educational Success. Another purpose of system building is for children to become productive citizens. Government documents that solicit proposals for the creation of early childhood systems, for example, reflect this view. This view is not ecologically based but rather focuses on children's academic trajectory from early childhood to adulthood.

These early childhood initiatives, such as the United States government's Race to the Top, aim to ensure that children enter elementary school prepared to succeed there. Their central purpose is to prepare children for academic success. Race to the Top offered incentives to

> provide continuity and consistent levels of care and education . . . that will
> have broad impact and can—

- Improve program quality and outcomes for young children;
- Increase the number of children with high needs attending high-quality early learning and development programs; and
- Help close the achievement gap between children with high needs and their peers by supporting efforts to increase kindergarten readiness (U.S. Department of Education, 2011, pp. 7–8).

Such school readiness initiatives have targeted continuity to maximize children's later ability to be productive citizens. The Department of Education is philosophically committed to preparing young children for their movement into elementary school. In short, such readiness initiatives create a system that includes early care and education in a vision for children from birth through college.

These two approaches to early childhood systems have significantly different goals. The ecological approach aims to improve the overall quality of life for children and families. The educational success approach uses early childhood care and education to keep children on track for future academic success. The ecological approach focuses on who children are now. The driving force behind the educational success approach, instead, is who they will become.

While early educators can create continuity when they link programs, if they do not attend to the nature of the programs they are connecting, the continuity may be undesirable. An early childhood system is a means to an end, whether that goal is improving children's and families' lives or promoting readiness for the next educational step. When creating a system itself becomes the goal, educators risk linking together programs that lack quality and do little to improve children's and families' lives (Klein, 2012) and are unlikely to achieve hoped-for goals.

Government funding initiatives such as Race to the Top, sources of philanthropic support from donors such as the Schumann Fund (supporting systems development in New Jersey), and advocacy efforts such as the Building Bridges campaign (sponsored by the American Academy of Pediatrics and early childhood partners from different states) aim to transform early childhood education from many fragmented and unconnected entities into a coordinated system. The Institute of Medicine and National Research Council (2015) points to

the essential need for consistency and continuity in early care and education both over time as children develop and across systems and services. Yet just when children would benefit most from high-quality experiences that build on each other consistently over time, the systems with which they interact are fragmented (p. 1).

In an effort to decrease fragmentation and increase continuity, states are fashioning systems. In the next section we look at four system-building movements or subsystems. Across the country, states implement these to varying degrees and in different ways.

Efforts to Create Continuity

Early childhood professionals have proposed numerous strategies to link existing partners into a single early childhood system that can provide continuity and coherence. One such strategy is to create subsystems that can operate independently or together: quality rating and improvement systems (QRIS), early professional development standards and systems, data systems, and early learning standards (Goffin, 2013; Klein, 2012; Ponder, 2012). At the foundation of each of these subsystems is the assumption of a shared core body of knowledge about how children grow and develop.

In this section you will read more about each of these subsystems:

- Quality practices promoted by QRIS
- The professional development that current and future teachers need
- The nature of the data educators and agencies collect and share
- Early learning standards appropriate for children

Those who design systems anticipate that successfully implementing these subsystems can positively support children's growth as the children move between settings. These subsystems can align practices across agencies and within systems.

Quality Rating and Improvement Systems (QRIS). Quality rating and improvement systems set criteria for and assess early childhood settings to improve and communicate about programs (Schaack, Tarrant, Boller, & Tout, 2012). Advocates believe that implementing a QRIS could improve the quality of early childhood settings and support early learning outcomes for children. This story from the coordinator of a local QRIS provides a picture of one QRIS in action.

Working for Change

It boggles my mind that programs can just put on a show. I was working as coordinator of a community quality rating and improvement system (QRIS) through our regional training and technical assistance program. Child care centers would volunteer to be part of this program. I would visit a center and work with the director, and everything would seem good. But then I would talk to parents who called our child care information and referral agency looking for a quality program. I'm talking up this program, and they'd say, "That's where my child is now, and this is not what I see." It was like the director was pretending just to put on a show for me.

QRIS assess staff qualifications or education, policies, practices, the learning environment, and the developmental appropriateness of the curriculum. Proponents of QRIS believe they encourage centers to improve their quality. QRIS describe high-quality practices that centers can emulate and, in some states, motivate centers with financial incentives to aim for that quality. As you can hear in the story "Working for Change," QRIS ostensibly provide families with information about the quality of the center. The parents in this story knew what they were seeing in the center and recognized that it was not quality.

QRIS raise the question of what quality early childhood education is and who decides. National organizations and the states themselves link higher QRIS ratings to their articulated ideas about quality. The ensuing standards—for example, those that encourage communication and understanding between home and school—may encourage practices that create continuity within the program. And QRIS that set standards across settings can create continuity for children who move between programs. Yet one definition of *quality* may not serve the purposes of all children, families, and teachers, thus generating discontinuity.

Professional Development and Degrees. Teacher education and training programs for pre- and inservice educators along with career lattices and degree attainment standards have become part of the work of building an early childhood system. The next story, from a community school administrator, illustrates how the combination of professional development and degree attainment coupled with insider knowledge of the local community contributes to continuity and a strong system.

The Parent Coordinator

Marisol was one of those active parents. She was the parent of three children in public schools in the community. She had come up from the Dominican Republic and was quite well educated there, but her credentials were not valid in the United States.

We saw Marisol's natural leadership qualities and hired her to work in the school as the parent coordinator. At that time, public schools did not have parent coordinators; we invented the role. We established a physical place where parents can be when they come to school. There's always coffee brewing, comfortable chairs, resources for getting jobs and finding housing, and workshops on being supportive of children's education and well-being. The parent coordinator's job is to reach out to families, help them feel welcome in school, and assess their needs and strengths to keep the program relevant. The parent coordinator literally coordinates activities for parents and other family members. We have a lot of active grandparents, and the parent coordinator reaches out to whoever a child's caregivers are. She helps them to feel comfortable and helps them with issues related to the children's education, their own education, and the family's well-being.

Twenty-three years later, Marisol is still the parent coordinator. She knows everybody in the community. She has—by being who she is—put herself through college. Although she already had a bachelor's degree from the Dominican Republic, when she saw it would not be accepted, she went back to school, got a second bachelor's and subsequently a master's. She has inspired so many other parents to go back to school and get a degree.

Based on Marisol and her work, when we hire a new parent coordinator, we look for a member of the community who has natural leadership ability and sees herself as a community builder. This kind of continuity is tremendously important. We tried to convince the public schools that this was the way to go, but instead they hire off the civil service list and have paid the price. In what passes for school reform, we forget how important relationships are in school buildings. The parent coordinator who is committed to the community is an example of continuity making a difference in the lives of children and families.

Standards for professional development aim to establish professional continuity by ensuring that each early childhood professional has a knowledge base about how children grow and develop and the best ways to support the child and family. Despite conflicting research on the impact of a teacher's credential or degree on children's learning and the difficulty of determining that impact, professional literature, teacher education programs, and professional organizations often promote degree attainment (Barnett, 2011; Institute of Medicine & National Research Council, 2015). For Marisol, this meant returning to college in the United States when the school did not recognize her Dominican credential.

In addition to formal education being of value, evidence points to the value of family and community funds of knowledge (González, Moll, & Amanti, 2005). As you read in Chapter 3, families know the cultural practices that influence their children's learning.

As early childhood systems emerge, the professionals who work in those systems will do their jobs best with a deep understanding of how children grow and how to support them and their families in these early years. As Marisol's story illustrates, real continuity within a system rests on leadership skills and commitment to the local community, not just on a degree or the core knowledge reflected in early learning standards and best practices. Successful intrasystemic continuity demands a relational disposition and the ability to build relationships. Marisol's role as a competent professional who sought additional education also served, through her relationships with parents and teachers, as a model for others to seek additional education. Relationships thus can promote a teacher's professional growth in powerful ways.

The next story is from a master teacher at a recently opened Early Head Start site. She provides professional development and supervision to the infant and toddler teachers.

The New Program

Last September, the teachers and children from an existing Early Head Start program came over to our new facility. The transition to our building was a sudden move for the teachers. They moved over here from their big, beautiful, ideal classrooms while our new space was still under construction. They had their children with them, and they felt protective of their children. That helped. Still, it was hard for them and for parents, too—moving was a huge disconnect.

In addition to the change of location, we were all new administrators for them. It was hard for them to trust us at first because they came from an environment where teachers were written up a lot for doing things wrong. There were a lot of rules to follow there, and the teachers felt like they were constantly in trouble. We've built in one-way mirrors, because we have a lot of visitors and don't want to disrupt the children's and teachers' day. At first, teachers were afraid of getting caught doing things wrong. Instead we try to be descriptive and respectful when we discuss observations. If we observe a difficult situation, we empathize and listen to the teacher's perspective.

From our very 1st week together, we started building relationships with the teachers, taking a strengths-based approach. We do a lot of listening to their stories to find out about their experiences and who they are. I went on home visits with the teachers and listened and learned about the community from them. In reflective supervision, we focus together on the children. I ask teachers to tell me about each of the children in their group and to ask one question about each child each week. I made a book about each teacher, with her picture, her philosophy, her background, and quotes from her. We spend a lot of time talking about what teachers do well and what they are working on with children and families. Time for supervision and observation—including through the one-way mirror—has made a big difference in our relationships. Now the teachers have attachments and relationships with the administrators, and we have a nice community despite their losing their old space. Doing classroom observations with time set aside to talk about them has made a big difference.

Here, new bonds with empathetic and caring administrators turned a potentially discontinuous situation into a learning opportunity—professional development—for teachers. Together, supervisors and teachers analyzed and reflected on the teachers' work with children in ways that supported the teachers. Once again, the ability to build continuity through relationships goes beyond having a degree. Personal qualities and a commitment to adult learning serve as the conduit for sharing knowledge.

An early childhood system thrives when the people in it are knowledgeable about children and constantly refresh that knowledge. This type of professional development infuses new energy and ideas for existing teachers. Meanwhile, teacher education programs generate a new pool of professionals for the system.

Data. Early childhood educators collect data in a variety of ways and for different reasons. As you will read in the next story, how educators use data varies, too.

Assessment in Pre-K and Kindergarten

This is an example of discontinuity. I've been a kindergarten teacher for many years, and this is my first year with pre-K. In pre-K, we use rubrics and you see a lot of gathering of observational data that provide developmental continuity. The fear is that when children leave pre-K and go to kindergarten, what happens to all this great documentation? I don't see a kindergarten teacher being able to use the same data *and* use all the data they have to use. If I were a kindergarten teacher, I could use it, but can they?

I use a lot of authentic gathering of documentation, portfolio installments, and observations. When children enter kindergarten, what happens to this authentic process? The systems for evaluation change to a more testing-like environment, for example, the DIBELS and Discovery. Some children demonstrate the typical skills and knowledge of a 5-year-old, and so it's very appropriate for those 5s. But I have some kids who aren't at that level yet. We don't do a testing environment to gather information in pre-K—we hear and observe their skills and abilities.

The coordinated collection and use of data constitute another subsystem in addition to QRIS and professional development. In this story, the lack of continuity within and across assessment and data collection systems troubles the teacher. She is concerned about sharing data over time and across grade levels. The types of assessment teachers use in kindergarten bother her, too. She worries on behalf of children who are not performing at the level the assessment requires. Moreover, many assessments do not provide information that helps teachers know each child well and develop responsive curriculum.

This story illustrates a significant obstacle for proponents of early childhood systems. Data that is useful for evaluating programs and schools may not be helpful to teachers. Data collection that is truly meaningful to teachers and for system building provides useful information for teaching along with continuity and coherence between settings, the data they collect, and the means they use to collect them. As the teacher in the assessment story above asks, "What happens to this authentic process?"—which she says she and other pre-K teachers use to assess children and inform their teaching.

Subsystems interconnect, interact, and have impact on each other. The following story from a teacher educator reveals complications that can arise because of the interconnected nature of this system.

What Is Really Important?

As in most states, if you want to be a teacher here you need to take a certification exam to show you know about children and the content you are going to teach. For elementary teachers, that includes a test that assesses your reading, math, science, and social studies and an art, music, and movement knowledge component. A while ago, I began to hear rumblings about the state removing the art, music, and movement questions from the test because the children in our schools weren't being tested in those areas. I was frustrated that everything was being determined by the proficiency tests the children were taking. If it wasn't on the test, it wasn't important.

Thankfully, with enough feedback and resistance from professionals in the field, they never enacted their proposition and kept art, music, and movement as content knowledge future teachers should know. But the power of that test to change everything in education worries me. I have heard colleagues say, "Reading is 30% of the test so we need to have two reading courses." I am certain that if art, music, and movement are removed from the test we will be pressured to drop those courses regardless of their impact on children's learning and development. Like dominoes falling in succession, K–12 assessments shape teacher certification exams, which, in turn, shape teacher preparation programs. If this is continuity, I am not sure I want it, because I value the arts—I value the social, emotional, and cognitive benefits children derive from moving and singing.

In this story, the state assesses future teachers based on what policymakers believe is important for children to learn. The data collection system influences the courses future teachers will take as part of their professional development. The teacher educator who told this story fears that tests will determine what teachers teach, in contrast to teaching based on what children are capable of and interested in learning.

States have developed early learning standards that outline what children know and can do at specific ages. What follows is the final subsystem: early learning standards.

Early Learning Standards. The next story describes a lack of consensus about children's capabilities and how best to support their development. It highlights the need for agreement about what children know and can do—a lacuna that early learning standards aim to fill.

Moving Downward on the Child

My story is about what I have been learning at school about the appropriate practices, especially for children under 5. I have worked in several child care centers and schools and I have found that many times what I have learned at school is not what is applied at centers, for example, what we, as caregivers, should be aware of regarding the child and his or her stage in development.

Currently, I am working with 4-year-olds and the expectations that the program is targeting (learning letters and basic math skills) do not match [the children]. I see children are in need of developing social and emotional skills—not through contracts, threats, or sitting isolated. Children need warm relationships and people (teachers) who actually love the idea of spending long hours with them and have the intention throughout the day to make a full rich experience for them. I believe love, fun, and learning should be the base of early childhood. We should plan learning that moves from the child (as an individual, knowing his or her needs) upward into the curriculum. What I see is that the schools move downward on the child with their curriculum.

The college student telling this story chafes under her program's expectations about when children acquire certain knowledge and skills, how teachers should support children's growth, and the teacher's consequent role in the classroom. These conflicting expectations lead to discontinuity. In response, states and agencies have established early learning standards that outline what abilities, skills, and knowledge teachers can expect from children at different ages. In the best of cases, early learning standards guide quality education and lead to assessments that generate data that accurately reflect children's strengths and inform ways to support further professional growth.

Early learning standards vary state by state but generally explain what to expect from children at different ages. They should be rooted in scientific research that takes into account human diversity. Well-conceived early learning standards have the potential to minimize inappropriate expectations. If, however, early learning standards are based on unrealistic expectations or do not reflect children's diverse ways of learning and being, they create a mismatch between what teachers do and who the children are. An early learning standard is an expectation for everyone. In the best-case scenario, these standards leave room for a range of children's behaviors. The differences between children can make a one-size-fits-all approach a poor fit for many.

Early learning standards also have the potential to link the expectations of children in one setting with what they will do in their next setting. This would be the case if, at the end of the year, a preschool teacher expected children to leave with the skills and knowledge their new kindergarten teacher anticipated that they would have. In fact, one reason to develop early learning standards is to link what children can or should do in the early years with what K–12 education expects of them. However, if either setting's standards do not reflect what diverse groups of children can or should do, discontinuity between the systems will result.

When settings, such as pre-K and kindergarten, have different views of children, early learning standards cannot resolve the difference, unless those who set curriculum for each setting work together. One solution is for kindergarten to share the child-centered values of most early childhood settings. Another, which "Moving Downward" questions, is for pre-K to become more like kindergarten and 1st grade. A third is for the two settings to negotiate with one another, understanding that preschool and kindergarten are not the same. Yet for a satisfactory outcome, advocates for preschool and for kindergarten must share a common language to be able to talk about children and how to teach them.

The stories teachers, directors, and teacher educators have shared illustrate the complexity associated with creating continuity for children and families through systems and subsystems. The stories that follow expand this complexity and illustrate why, despite all efforts to support continuity for children through system building, continuity remains elusive.

What Really Creates Continuity and Discontinuity?

The people who develop early childhood systems aim for continuity. Systems that achieve continuity include an ongoing process of negotiating philosophical consensus and cohesion. In addition, successful systems are flexible enough to allow for a variety of local applications.

Consensus and Cohesion. Building continuity into an early childhood system is particularly challenging because early childhood educators at every level, from assistant teachers to policymakers, have historically lacked consensus and cohesion. The next story shows how such philosophical discontinuity appears in the everyday lives of children, teachers, and families.

The Bearer of Bad News

I sit in Head Start leadership meetings and we really believe in the importance of parents. We discuss expectations and the importance of communication about their child's learning. We do everything—even drive parents to doctor's appointments. But one thing that we don't do well is prepare parents for the public schools. We prepare the kids but not their parents. I guess we don't want to be the bearer of bad news. . . . The families leave us and go to public schools and have no idea what's going to happen. They have to be buzzed in the front door of the school and then interrogated by the receptionist: "Why are you here?" The public schools won't spend 20 minutes talking to the family. It's not welcoming. They don't invite conversation like Head Start. The family piece just drops off in the public schools.

This Head Start education coordinator describes two school cultures that differ dramatically. Articulated and unspoken philosophies underlie each system's practices. While the public schools in this community do not intend to be unwelcoming, somehow they are. Collaboration with families does not hold the priority there that it does in Head Start. This results in discontinuous experiences for families and leaves the professional who offered this story feeling remorseful for not preparing them.

Kagan and Tarrant (2010) point to differing philosophies for working with and caring for children. Philosophical discontinuities have "bequeathed a fragmented landscape for young children, their families and the myriad institutions that serve them" (p. 8). This fragmentation can preclude smooth transitions between programs for children and families.

Different settings have different approaches and aims. To reach consensus, representatives of programs and agencies join together and look for points of intersection. Consensus implies that everyone has a voice at the table. In conversation with one another the parties arrive at agreement about what seems best for children and families at that particular time. The different professional backgrounds, orientations, and purposes of different agencies can make communication difficult. Thus, consensus demands an intentional effort at ongoing dialogue and negotiation. Since children and contexts change perpetually, to work, systems must adapt with them.

Flexibility for Local Applications. The people who create systems are rarely the ones who implement them. Sometimes systems produce unanticipated effects, as one master teacher told us.

Figuring It All Out

We have a center-based program here and a home-based program that is based at another site. When we had a federal review, we didn't know what the others were doing. Now one person heads both, having taken over the grant. It's a huge job for that person to be involved with everything: the local funding source; universal pre-K; the licensing agency; Early Head Start; and partnering with the local public school for the physical operations of our program, including school safety, facilities, and food. On top of that we're also part of a big nonprofit and have grants from foundations. We're figuring it all out.

Sometimes the systems we work with come into conflict with each other. For example, Head Start requires teachers to sit with children and eat during meals. Our food comes from the public school that houses us, and the school won't provide food for the adults—just for the children. So the teachers sit with the children, but they don't eat.

This center offers multiple services to children of different ages and blends various funding streams. Bringing together a range of resources, the center can create continuity for children and families over time as children move from Early Head Start into preschool and on to a class in the public school, all in the same building. Yet since the center is accountable to different agencies, it faces discontinuity when outsiders assess the center's work and on a daily basis when the rules of one part of the system conflict with the requirements of another. The comprehensive and potentially continuous services that this agency can offer are one of its strengths. At the same time, they create some of its greatest difficulties.

Here is an example of how policies, based on what should work, can create unforeseen consequences when administrators and teachers apply them in their local settings. A challenge, then, to those hoping to create continuity through an overarching system, is to allow flexibility for site-specific situations that no one who is apart from that context could anticipate.

WHAT COMPLICATES CONTINUITY

Early educators are far from agreeing upon a vision of one comprehensive early childhood system (Scott, 2012) or how to go about achieving it. In the following sections, you will read about variables that complicate continuity and philosophical divergences that make cohesion and consensus difficult to achieve.

Four Variables

Kagan (2010) proposes that four variables contribute to discontinuity within the field: temporal variables, disciplinary variables, institutional variables, and contextual variables. Juggling these variables poses a challenge for early educators. *Temporal variables* arise from the many biological, physical, and intellectual changes children undergo during their 1st years of life. Consider the vast differences between infants, preschoolers, and elementary-age children.

For a center to meet the needs of children and families throughout the early childhood years, practitioners must draw upon many disciplines, including mental health, nutrition, family studies, child development, and educational theory. These *disciplinary variables* create situations in which professionals with different preparation work together. They come from different orientations, have different foci and values, and may use different professional vocabularies.

Institutional variables include the family and the school or center. Funding sources, government agencies, and religious institutions may oversee a center's work. The center is accountable to each, with each one's separate and conceivably conflicting requirements.

Contextual variables refer to the larger picture in which early childhood education operates. Thanks to brain research and advocacy on the part of early educators, some policymakers and government officials have become aware of early care and education in new ways and become new partners in early education. Such contextual variables can enable a center to merge funding streams and set up a multi-age program.

The people who work in an early childhood system juggle at least some of these variables. If the policymakers who design the systems do not take these variables, among others, into consideration, systems risk discontinuity that can negatively affect local programs.

Philosophical Stances

Playing for the First Time

When Eli went home from the rehabilitation center where he spent the 1st year of his life, I began to visit him as his developmental interventionist. My approach was very different from the tests and therapies that he was used to in rehab.

   Although his motor skills and stamina were quite limited, in one of the first sessions I offered him a stick to hold on to. He took the stick and I held up a drum. When he moved the stick I would move the drum so they would connect and make a sound. His face lit up and soon he was banging and giggling, which turned into belly laughing. His mom had tears coming down her face as she said, "He's playing!" This was one of the first times he was in charge of the play. No one was moving his hand or making something happen for him. He was playing, and it was pure joy.

A specialist in early intervention with a strong early childhood background told us this story. It illustrates how early childhood practitioners from disparate disciplines differ in their perceptions of children and in their approaches to interactions with them. These philosophical differences begin to explain why creating continuity within early childhood systems is so challenging and why it is not always desirable.

   The "Playing for the First Time" story describes how equally well-educated providers from different disciplines, but within the same early care system, approach children in different ways, yet both support the child's growth. The author of this story believes that the child is inherently capable of learning when play strategies match his abilities and desires. She facilitates the child's actions and enables him in his play. In contrast, the professionals at the rehabilitation center worked to move him along a trajectory they had in mind while measuring his progress, as was their job. Philosophical beliefs and professional preparation undergird work with children. This story sheds light on how different professional perspectives can complicate continuity within early childhood systems but can also work in tandem as separate pieces of the same system.

   Early childhood education is a complicated field. In addition to the factor of its multidisciplinarity, governmental and nongovernmental agencies hold oversight and wield power. Each agency has a mission that drives decisions about where to put energy and funding—decisions that affect children, families, and teachers at the local level.

Early childhood is "housed" in multiple national, state, and local legislative departments. This is a systems issue, as policies, professional requirements, and philosophies differ for each entity and vary state to state. Larger entities—the national, state, and local legislative departments that make early childhood policy, for example—differ philosophically as well. Each has jurisdiction over early learning standards, definitions of quality, professional development and trainings, and data collection. What they ask of programs may differ, creating conflicts when early childhood programs are accountable to more than one of these entities. Furthermore, philosophical approaches to early childhood may differ from state to state.

Views of Children. Philosophical beliefs shape core knowledge and thereby further define what professionals do to help children grow and learn. In the stories below, we continue to see how philosophical differences influence continuity.

Never His Strengths

John had two years in preschool—two different teachers and settings, but similar in philosophy. John's first setting was a public school preschool for children with disabilities, but all the other children were only speech delayed. Next was his pre-K classroom at a university lab school. There were 20 kids, and John did well. It was a great experience, because there were so many model children for John. It was a seamless transition between these two different institutions.

Then we transitioned John to public school for kindergarten. There weren't the warm, friendly, nurturing people we were used to. The transition was hard on John and me. The systems were different! First there were all the evaluations and observations John had to go through! The occupational therapist was terrible! She had no people skills. Those people didn't know him—they pointed out all his "deficiencies" to me. Never his strengths . . . and I was used to people telling me about John's developing strengths.

In this story the parent experienced continuity when she and the teachers focused together on John's capabilities. When he transitioned to a new setting and the teachers emphasized his "deficiencies," the discontinuity between the teachers' and the parent's ways of viewing John created a hard transition for both parent and child. This intense discontinuity occurred despite such transition activities as visiting the new school.

This story illustrates the impact of philosophical differences on continuity. The family had to change their expectations. The mother continued, recalling:

> There were times I wanted to take him out. But I didn't really have a choice because he was old enough for kindergarten. I had to change my expectations of a classroom. I had to decide if it could be good enough and then adjust to move forward.

Fortunately, John and his family regained continuity. His mother concluded, "Now I understand the teacher and what she wants from John . . . and she sees John as a capable child." As this story shows, individual teachers take strength-based and deficit perspectives depending on their own orientations.

How Children Learn. In addition to holding different views of children, early childhood educators disagree about how children learn best. Classroom arrangements, materials, and teacher–child interactions speak to different pedagogical approaches that are based on views of how children learn.

Squelched

I was a public school kindergarten teacher and I'm thinking about the difference between the pre-K setting and kindergarten. So the children leave their pre-K with the playing they do there. Although we're early childhood educators, too, there's the expectation that we have to put forth, in the first 2 weeks of school, the testing and assessment in kindergarten.

We used this computerized test, but the children just wanted to play with the mouse. Children wanted to explore the environment and couldn't care less about the assessment task on the screen, yet we were using that data to gauge our instruction. The lack of continuity between where they came from (pre-K) and what we were doing was so abrupt.

A little boy who was being raised by his grandmother and had very limited prior experience with computers came into kindergarten. He was instructed to sort striped balls into one basket and polka-dot balls in the other basket on his computer screen. This was just one of 25 questions he was "supposed" to answer. I watched as he played with those balls, putting all in one basket and then back in the other basket. He was not going to move past that one question, because he was so fascinated by moving those bright colored balls on the computer screen. I can remember the pressure I was feeling watching him, knowing that his exploration was going to ultimately have a negative outcome in the form of a nonproficient test score and feeling so torn on how I could best support him in this situation. I encouraged him to move on to the next question, which was not nearly as intriguing, as it was a written passage read aloud to him which then asked him some type of comprehension question. And with that I had squelched his exploration.

This kindergarten teacher values play and child-directed exploration, as do many early childhood educators. The National Association for the Education of Young Children (2009) identifies both as essential elements of Developmentally Appropriate Practices. The story highlights the clash between those values and the assessment-driven culture in which this teacher works.

This story echoes the discontinuity between pre-K and kindergarten that you read about in an earlier story, "Assessment in Pre-K and Kindergarten." Both teachers value the child as an individual and strive to create environments that afford flexibility and are responsive to the individual child. Both describe kindergarten settings that use standardized assessments.

Teachers and parents told us that continuity between home and school requires the ongoing navigation of transitions and new relationships. To support children and families through times of discontinuity, programs can familiarize families and children with the culture of the school, provide consistent expectations between home and school, and help children and families feel ownership of the school. For example, they can organize meetings between previous teachers, future teachers, and parents to discuss expectations of the new setting. Parents or preschool teachers can take children to see their kindergarten classroom before the school year begins. Teachers can collaborate to ensure that their curriculum builds on what the children learned the previous school year.

Nonetheless, even the best transition activities cannot bridge philosophical discontinuity between the pre-K and K–12 systems. Even thoughtful ways to ease children into a new setting may fail to address fundamental philosophical differences between systems. These differences preclude continuity and cause many early childhood educators to question whether they want continuity that means acquiescing to a philosophical view so different from their own.

Teacher's Role. In the story above, the teacher experienced discontinuity between what she believed was best for children and how she saw her role as a teacher. However, even when two parts of an organization or system presumably hold similar philosophical beliefs about children, differences in how members of the system perceive the teacher's role affect the continuity of the child's experience and learning.

Kicked Out

A parent enrolled in our Early Head Start home visitor program prenatally. When the baby was a year old, she began attending our center-based program and remained with us until she was 3½. Throughout that time she stayed with the same teachers.

At first, the mom had a hard time getting out of bed to get her daughter to school. It was difficult for her to set goals for her child. Our family worker and she set up a time-management plan. They met regularly, and the family staff exchanged information with the teachers about the child's development and what was happening with the family. From the time she started Early Head Start until the time she left for our agency's Head Start program, we could see the growth of both the family and the child.

The teachers felt empowered. Through collaboration with the family workers, they could see that they played a role in the child's success in the program. At first, they described the child's disorganized behavior, but as the child got older and as her mother became more organized, the teachers said the child demonstrated fewer challenging behaviors.

When she left the program, her teachers thought she was ready for pre-K. They had no concerns. When she went to Head Start, the Early Head Start staff told the Head Start staff about the child and the family and what we did to achieve success with them. The mom had another child who attended our Early Head Start program, which meant we stayed in touch with the mom about her first child's experience in Head Start. Her first child now had an IEP. She was aggressive. Her behavior went in the opposite direction from the way it had gone in Early Head Start. It seemed to us to be a program issue. Whenever we met with the Head Start staff, they complained about her behavior. For kindergarten, her mom enrolled her in a charter school, but the child was expelled for hitting her teacher.

We had continuity of care in Early Head Start, but there was a disconnect between Early Head Start and Head Start within the same agency—although there was not supposed to be. We were supposed to have continuity in delivery of service as well.

In Early Head Start, the teachers collaborated with other professionals to support the child and mother. As the child transitioned to Head Start and especially to the charter school, the teachers there expected certain behaviors from her and identified problems when she did not comply.

This story tells of two programs in the same agency that, despite common policies, educational criteria, and an articulated mission that values families, were unable to provide continuity for this family.

The author of "Kicked Out" talks about discontinuity that existed within an agency. In addition, perceptions of the teacher's role differ across agencies. The next story illustrates a case of discontinuity between two separate systems that ostensibly work hand in hand: higher education that prepares teachers and the schools where the teachers will work.

All That Thinking

I've noticed a disconnect between what we ask of teacher candidates in higher education and what schools ask of teachers. Curriculum and planning is scripted in the public school, and each school is different. They have their own curriculum that teachers follow that asks them only for a couple of sentences in terms of a lesson plan. I'm asking for full-length lesson plans. They have to follow a long guideline for lesson plans that includes accommodations and an actual description of what they're doing, connections to prior learning, and assessment of learning—so that we know that they know. The college students want to know why they have to do all that thinking and learning when they are not going to use it in their professional lives. I tell them, you may go to a school that doesn't use a scripted curriculum, in which case you will have to know how to plan curriculum.

This story tells of the discontinuity between a teacher education program's view of the teacher's role as a thinker and planner and the school district's view of a teacher as one who implements a script someone else has designed. The college student is caught in the middle. In an effort to create continuity for children, many schools have adopted scripted curriculum and districtwide scope and sequence. These efforts may result in consistency between classrooms but may not create continuity for the child for whom that curriculum is a poor fit or for teachers who cannot use their pedagogical skills.

TENSION WITHIN THE MICRO AND MACRO LEVELS

This chapter has addressed system planning at the policy level and system implementation at the local level. In this final section, we examine how these macro and micro levels interact with each other.

In the next story, a nursery school director describes how an accreditation review—an element of the macro level—drew the director's attention to the micro level of the small system that was their school.

Classrooms Within Schools

There was an issue of continuity between classes at our school. We talked a lot about separation from home but not from classrooms. It seems so obvious and simple that they could have done the same songs as the children did in their previous class, but there wasn't a lot of openness to considering this, because everyone was really set in their classroom's programs.

The school was known to be a close, nurturing environment, sensitive to children's needs, and the teachers had been there forever. It was like a second home to the teachers. So you would think the teachers would be close and working together.

My knowledge of this discontinuity grew out of the accreditation process and the staff answers on the questionnaire. Several teachers commented that they didn't know what other classes were doing and that they felt there was a lack of sharing and connection between classes. What seemed like snarky comments at the time revealed a negative climate in the school. The evaluator pointed out that there was little communication on a professional level between teachers and that there was resentment and competition. There really wasn't continuity between the classrooms. Teachers talked to each other about the children and what they had done to help a particular child, but communicating about curriculum was a whole new area that needed a lot of work.

We can do the whole thing between home and school, but we haven't looked *within* the schools. These comments from the staff questionnaire led to discussions about how to strengthen connections and improve the climate in the school. It led to a shift in our focus at staff meetings to one of sharing from within much more frequently.

These teachers understood children's development and how to plan curriculum that matched the child's knowledge and skills. They demonstrated quality practices by providing continuity during transitions between their program and children's prior and future experiences and between home and school. Yet the teachers did not communicate or collaborate about their teaching to create curricular continuity for children throughout the school. While the teachers held a common philosophy and approach to children, they did not share the specifics that made up the children's daily lives.

This story illuminates that building continuity into a guiding sub-system (for example, early learning standards or a QRIS) is insufficient. According to this director, in addition to nurturing continuity in each transition between agencies, the educators who work within the same system have the power and responsibility to create continuity within that system as well. The teachers in the preceding story began communicating with one another about their work to achieve continuity for children moving from room to room. Their relationships with each other made the difference. The story highlights the many influences on curricular continuity, including the teachers themselves.

Relationships at the Micro Level

Despite efforts to establish transitions across contexts, create continuity within the curriculum and across grades through early learning standards, and improve the quality of early care and education through a QRIS and shared data, teacher's stories reflect complexity. Early educators spoke to us of their efforts to help children connect one moment to the next and enable children to expand an experience as they move on.

Coming Home

My program starts with children who are from 20 months to 2 years. Parents were interested in more than that. We now serve 2s, 3s, and 4s and even walk children to and from the local public pre-K. Children go to their new "big school," but remain in our program for the parts of the day when there is no public school.

This story is from a family child care provider who runs what she says began as a "preschool playgroup." Once the children go on to the public schools for a 2-hour and 20-minute session, staff from her program provide support for the new school, as she says, "with continuity with us." The children seem able to "come home" to her program even as they take a small taste of "big school." The program is like a nest to which the children can return after venturing out. It provides context for the children's new school experience.

In this story, continuity enables the children to go out into the world in small steps because of teacher–child relationships at the "little school." The little school is not necessarily communicating with the big school or adhering to the same quality or professional standards. It nonetheless facilitates the children's transition and connection to their new experiences in the "big school." The micro-level relationships at the little school enabled children to experience continuity as they ventured out. Looking back at all these stories, you can see how teachers develop continuity within the system at the micro level and that, as Dewey (1938/1997) maintains, one experience enables the next to be more and more educative.

System-building work occurs at the macro level through policies and procedures. Teachers enact those policies and procedures on the micro level through daily interactions with children, families, and the other early childhood professionals who work with them. Policymakers can plan for continuity at the systems or macro level, but as the stories that follow show, policy intentions are often quite different from the everyday outcomes that result. The system-building work at the macro level then can inhibit continuity at the micro level where individual children, teachers, and families connect one experience to the next.

The next story talks about how teachers resist that tension between the micro level at which they operate and the macro level that monitors them.

We Don't Get Freaked Out

We've decided not to be freaked out by everyone who comes in to assess us. In fact, sometimes it's hard to remember who wants what.

With the help of consultants and our director, we're bringing everything together based on Powerful Interactions and its three-step process for building relationships with children (paying attention to your own feelings so you can be fully present for the child, using observations of the child to know the child and communicate interest in the child, thus deepening the relationship and extending the child's experiences based on this relationship). It's given us the time to observe, connect, reflect, and be incredibly open. It's given us strong guiding principles.

This teacher refers to strong guiding principles that focus on relationship (Dombro, Jablon, & Stetson, 2011). They form the basis for continuity despite great discontinuity in the systems she and her colleagues negotiate on a daily basis.

Standardization at the Macro Level

Sadly, our stories also warn of the risks associated with practices and policies that attempt to establish sameness rather than foster strong relationships and connection. The challenge is to develop systems in which the key players remain decisionmakers and can tailor their teaching to the children and families with whom they work. Otherwise, we can fall prey to a false continuity that embodies sameness and singular ways. Although a frequent result of efforts to develop continuity, standardization is not continuity. Standardization, as the story below illustrates, inhibits the connections that continuity can provide.

Bundles

What I normally see in the schools I visit is teachers going crazy unpacking the bundles. Bundles are packages from the Department of Education or from the district. This is the social studies bundle; this is the math bundle; this is the literacy bundle. The social studies bundle might be "my community." And this is what all kindergarteners are going to be studying in that district. First-graders are going to be studying whatever. It's the old story of having a big theme, but they give lots of requirements that you have to meet. This comes to the school, and they have to start doing that, like, next week. So the teachers are all of a sudden in this position where many of them know, deep down inside, how to get there; but the way it's posed makes them completely spin trying to meet those requirements. And to me, this is completely wrong.

I remember one particular 1st-grade classroom. It was social studies. The teacher of the class was sitting behind his laptop showing images on the smart board of ancient Mesopotamia, of the Hammurabi Code and the importance of agriculture for the survival of that community. This was in the South Bronx in November and many of these children had not turned 6 years old. That was the introduction, the first time the teacher was talking about it. A few minutes into the smart board presentation, there was probably one child who was still looking at the smart board. There were children in the closet, throwing things, dumping math manipulatives—and the poor teacher didn't know what to do. Thankfully, the bell rang and the children were escorted to the gym or somewhere else. The teacher was embarrassed, and we started talking. I asked him if he knew what Mesopotamia means. He said, yes, "two rivers." The Bronx has rivers, too. Do the children know about the rivers near the Bronx? Have they ever been to the rivers? Probably not. What's agriculture? Let's look at the Bronx. Is there agriculture there? What about Hammurabi and his code? Did they have a chance to create their own classroom code? Everything is packed into 45 minutes. I asked him what he'd like to follow up with on this lesson, and he said, "Well, that was it. Next week we're going to be talking about ancient China."

The expectation that—especially in the early elementary years— children will conform to a mandated curriculum and goals is ludicrous. It is not consistent with what we know about learning, which is that people learn better and more deeply when they are invested in the topic, in the experiences, and when their curiosity is encouraged. I think that right now we do see a big example of not taking into consideration that development is continuous and that things don't happen all of a sudden. They may be noticed all of a sudden, but things have been happening below the surface. So, planning and implementing curriculum has to come from the children and not from someone "out there."

Our challenge, then, is to create an early childhood system that does not seek sameness in the name of continuity. Uniformity or standardization mandated at the macro level prevents interaction and adaptation on the micro level. Rather, the early childhood system must seek ways to build connections that nurture individual relationships, because these relationships enable children and families to be known by the agencies and professionals with whom they interact. This knowledge and understanding is essential to helping children expand on past experiences and contexts as they continue to grow and learn.

CHAPTER 5

Continuity and Professional Identity
Putting on My Teacher Hat

A Transformation

I remember beginning my work in a lab preschool. It was approaching naptime. I asked what the routines were and was informed that each child was to be read a book and then we were to rub or pat the child's back until they fell asleep. My first thought was, "Are you kidding me? Don't you just tell them to get on their cot and go to sleep?" I could not believe that two to three people were going to have to do this for 14 children, nor did I believe it would be possible to get all 14 children down so that everyone was actually asleep at the same time (and trust me, as much as we love our jobs, we really wanted all children down). The task seemed unmanageable and absurd in some ways. Having to do it felt like discontinuity. I felt like saying, "This is messed up." But, ultimately, this is what I was getting paid for so I did it.

In the process, something magical happened. Over time, experience created a transformation, a paradigm shift, where I learned tactics that helped me connect with each child in different ways, which had me eventually and confidently saying, "I know what to do to get this one down" (and quickly, might I add). Creating such connections forced me to stop and evaluate the basis of my prior thinking. Not only did my relationships with each child grow; I learned to value the individualized time that I had with each child as I read to them and patted them to sleep. The naptime process helped me get to know each child better and to create stronger bonds with them, which led me to wonder, what is the next thing I will encounter that is going to throw a wrench in my practices?

Although this educator had been a child care provider for many years, the move to a new setting "felt like discontinuity." Here, as you read in previous chapters, discontinuity provides a chance to rethink and change perspective and perhaps alter practices. And in a teacher's doing so, his or her continuously evolving identity as a professional transforms.

As we listened to stories of continuity and discontinuity related to early educators' identities, we saw a complex and continuous process that involved plenty of discontinuity as well. Trust and comfort figure largely in stories of identity development and the continuity or discontinuity inherent in that process. Interestingly, stories of power, whether the educator felt powerful or powerless, became stories of discontinuity. Philosophical alignment with colleagues and with early childhood ideology led some educators to experience continuity. Others described misalignment and discontinuity. Philosophical divergence entertains a diversity of ideas and approaches that both enriches practice and can discomfit practitioners. Finally, educators spoke about personal identities that differentiate them from stereotypical images of early childhood educators. All their stories revealed insights and raised questions about continuity, discontinuity, and early childhood identities.

THE CONTINUOUS AND DISCONTINUOUS NATURE OF DEVELOPING AN IDENTITY

The teacher who told us the "Transformation" story brings her identity and experience as a parent to her work. As she engages in the work itself, she combines her personhood with her practice. This process is not necessarily linear and involves both continuity and discontinuity.

Merging Identities

Cabral (2012) discusses three coexisting yet different aspects to teachers' identities. The three potentially can create discontinuity for teachers, as they did for the teacher in this chapter's opening story. The first is *personal identity*, which situates teachers within their own families and communities. In "A Transformation," the storyteller was a parent of several children and could not imagine rubbing children's backs instead of sending them off to bed. The second is *professional identity*, which is related to the roles and responsibilities of a teacher such as those that she adopted in her new setting. The third is a *teaching identity*, an image of who one is as an educator. One constructs that complex and dynamic teaching identity over time. She refers to her teaching identity when she talks about a paradigm shift. It is not dependent on her roles and responsibilities but rather is a sense of vocation.

A man who spoke to us about his experience as an early childhood educator in Head Start demonstrates Cabral's three coexisting aspects of a teacher's identity and adds another dimension as well.

Gotta Fix My Kid

You stick out when you're a man in early childhood, and that's great. Parents look at a male and seem to think, "Yes, that's what I want. Gotta fix my kid." They want me to be a man in their child's life.

But it changes when you're an administrator. Folks see you and say, "You're a great teacher; you should be an administrator." I go to director meetings and I'm still one of only five men in a room filled with women. There continues to be not enough men in the field.

I kind of like the idea of being a male in the field who is trying to support more men. Shortly after I was employed here, there was an explosion of more men working here. The program is always looking to bring in more males. I don't know if I was the catalyst, but I feel good about the important role I play in the classroom, as an administrator, and in this field.

This early childhood educator brings his identity as a man to his work in the classroom. As a professional he does what early childhood educators do. His teaching identity is that of a man in early childhood who listens carefully to and nurtures children, often providing an image of a man that is different from what some of the children experience at home. From what this teacher tells us, the mothers value their children's daily interactions with a reliable and caring man.

Yet his story also demonstrates the way in which Cabral's identities operate in a larger context. Stereotypical views of men and women direct men toward administrative roles. A man is the one who can "fix my kid." His story is a reminder to look beyond personal, professional, and teaching identities to the societal issues that surround them. Identity exists in sociopolitical contexts.

Fluid and Flexible Identities

Teachers are inevitably members of multiple communities. Their home lives, roots, education, and past and current practice result in different aspects of their multilayered identities. These context-dependent identities are flexible (Letts & Simpson, 2003) and fluid (Warren, 2014). One's teaching identity changes as circumstances change.

Developing one's teaching identity involves making sense of one's practice and of daily life with children (Wenger, 1998), a process that is neither stable nor simple (Alsup, 2006). Teachers and directors negotiate their teaching identities in the context of their communities of children, colleagues, and families. In the next story, a director described how she changed as she learned from the local community where she worked.

Adaptation

We have a lot of children now who are witnessing repeated violence, and we have a tremendous, a shocking amount of domestic violence going on. We've always had neighborhood violence, but since the recession, there's been a rise in domestic violence. We've had to make a much more therapeutic program than I anticipated having. As a result there's a lot more structure. I can't believe I see preschoolers lining up to go into the gym. I never thought I would find myself asking teachers to do that. So much is an adaptation to what children are used to from their home environments.

There's too huge a gap and not enough bridge building between the free play mentality we have in school and what the children's experiences are in a world of compliance made necessary by the context. We try to find what makes sense to the children, to balance what provides the structure and rigidity that compliance asks of them in the rest of their lives with developing inner control and self-regulation. How we bridge the two is a constant discussion, a constant trial and error. We advertise ourselves as play based, but children have to make a plan before going from point A to point B. But the child is able to move from point A to point B because we've given that structure.

Although we cannot generalize about children and families living in poverty, in this director's experience the children thrive on more rules and structure than she was inclined to offer. In reflection with others, she sought ways to bridge the children's home and school experiences. She also juggled her identity as a play-based educator with one who wanted to make school work for the children. Her willingness to study the children led to a shift in her teaching approach and thus in her identity. She never thought she would have children lining up, but it seemed to help them. She did it, although it challenged her picture of herself as an educator.

Such flexibility through reflective practice supports the development of a teaching identity. Reflective practice, especially in a social context, leads to growth and subsequent changes in teaching identity (Hung, 2008). As you saw in "Adaptation," colleagues help each other think.

TRUST, COMFORT, AND CONTINUITY

When early childhood educators thought about continuity and talked about their identities and roles as educators, they told us about feeling secure in their interactions with others and being trustworthy themselves. They also described experiences of when they did not feel trust or comfort.

The Leader's Identity as Trustworthy (or Not)

Next, we examine how leaders perceive their identities, and how they influence identity formation for those with whom they work. In the following story, a principal shared her reaction when she believed her educational community needed her. In her telling, she emphasized that her actions represent who she is and wants to be as an educational leader.

The Actions We Take

I was sitting on a small puddle jumper in Bloomington, Illinois. I had been a principal for just 6 months. Before the plane took off, I got a call from the assistant principal. My toddler teacher had passed away that morning. I sat on the plane absorbing the news. Finally permitted to disembark, I sped to Champaign, Illinois, and spent the rest of my day breaking the news to parents and consoling staff members. I wanted parents to hear the news from the school—from me—first.

In this age of Facebook and instant messaging, the rules of communication have changed, and dealing with people face to face is easily avoidable. Yet when I think about continuity in the early childhood community, I think about interaction and the trust families place in their child care providers.

For me, trust is built based on the actions we take when faced with challenges, questions, and uncertainty. I cannot say I said all the right words in exactly the right way during this time of uncertainty in my school community, but I was there, willing to share, feel, and give a hug to anyone who needed it.

The continuity in this story stems from the principal's view of herself as a member of the early childhood community in which she worked. In her story, she pointed to the continuity between the identity she constructed for herself as a new principal and the steps she took to shape that identity in the midst of this crisis.

Mentors are also leaders. They listen and advise, are trustworthy and comforting. In the next story, a teacher told us how her continuous relationship with a mentor affected her teaching identity.

The Oak Tree

I student taught in the 1960s with someone who was not just a teacher. She was and is also a political activist. There was a lot of antiwar stuff going on at the time, and we were both part of a group who went to Washington to protest the Vietnam War. We bonded. She became my mentor and has been with me every step of the way. Now she's 92 and is still as sharp as a whip.

She's still my mentor. I remember when I took leave from a job; she sat with me and weighed the pros and cons about leaving it or going back to it. She's been my oak tree. She embodies the best of progressive pedagogy that I learned in graduate school. She made me the strong teacher I think I am and have been. There are many other teachers I had, too, but she's *it* for my working, professional self. And now I'm that for other people, students I've taught about early childhood education.

Throughout her career, this teacher educator has found stability and continuity in her mentor's leadership and support. Their philosophical congruence as progressive educators enhanced their ability to reflect meaningfully together on work with children.

Early childhood educators take ideological positions that they enact throughout their work with children and families. These two stories contrast with two others we heard about discontinuity and leaders' identities. When the leadership does not support a teacher's ideological position, discontinuity can ensue.

The next story recalls an experience early in a teacher's career when the foundations of her professional ideas were already in place. She was nonetheless vulnerable when the administration of her new job did not support her work.

Something Wrong with Me

After working with people who shared my philosophy of teaching, I took a job at a private school, subbing for a teacher who didn't come back after spring break. After some negotiations, I agreed to return the following year.

In this school, no one shared much about each other's classrooms. The kindergarten teachers came in wearing high heels and talked to everyone through clenched teeth. Expectations of children were based on what they would need to know much later, and no one understood child development. The director had no pedagogy of her own and said yes to whatever she thought parents wanted to hear. She said she wanted me and child-centered early childhood education, but my classroom was completely different from everyone else's.

I started to feel as if there was something wrong with me. It was a hard year for me. I was going to leave teaching, but then I heard about an opening at another school. I applied and got the job and was back in the groove of talking about kids and education. I no longer felt insane. At the other school I was odd woman out. I thought it was me. If they had had a clear pedagogy of their own, I could have seen it wasn't a good match.

Without consistency and clarity from the leadership, this teacher became uncomfortable. She could not trust what the administrator said or did, and the teacher's identity was upended. Once she reflected upon her observations—no curriculum sharing, apparently unhappy teachers not dressed to play with children, and nothing in common between her classroom and the others—she realized that nothing was wrong with her. She was then able to see that instead this setting was not right for her and threatened rather than supported her professional identity.

The next story tells about three different principals and how their directive, supportive, or erratic styles affected the teachers in their schools.

Administrative Styles

I worked at three different schools as a kindergarten teacher. The population of each school reflected a different socioeconomic status, and I noticed a definite difference in leadership styles of administrators.

The first school I worked at had a strong administrator. She commanded respect, and most of the staff feared her displeasure, adhered to her deadlines, and respected her.

The second administrator was more flexible and very insightful. She truly cared for her teachers, and I can't say I felt that way about the first principal. I was also a more seasoned teacher by that 3rd year when I started with this second school. There were fewer deadlines, but still deadlines. There was more room for creativity in teaching to evolve. The biggest difference in the first two schools was the more relaxed nature of the second school.

Unlike at the previous two schools, the administrator at the third school rarely had deadlines. Staff often spoke badly behind her back. I was surprised by how disrespectful teachers could be. It was a struggle for me to feel part of the school culture, even though I tried. The lack of communication between administration and faculty permeated the instructional teams. Professional development was much less available than before, and the workload increased, too.

According to this teacher, an administrator creates (or does not) a climate of trust and comfort. Without support both tangible and intangible, this teacher felt a sense of discontinuity. Disconnecting from the school community, she could not work with children in as satisfying a way, which colored her identity as a teacher in that school.

In all these stories, early childhood leadership proves essential. In the first story, the school leader felt continuity with the rest of her school and made an effort to be present for them. In the second, the mentor created continuity for her mentee. The last two stories provide counter examples. In the third story, leadership that was chameleon-like left a teacher at loose ends. The final story described three principals, one of whom was authoritarian, while another was disorganized. Both caused a teacher to feel at a loss and disconnected. For these last two storytellers, the teaching experience became discontinuous, and teaching identity was put off balance.

Professional Roles

As Wenger (1998) puts it, "Who we are lies in the way we live day to day" (p. 151). These daily practices establish the roles educators adopt throughout their careers. They may feel varying degrees of comfort in each. Katz (2013) discusses how unclear the role boundaries are for those who work with young children in contrast to older children. The responsibilities are extensive: from toileting and feeding to promoting executive functions to teaching children to master current technology. As one's early childhood teaching identity evolves, one learns to live within the unclear boundaries.

Identity itself is a trajectory, journey, and set of transitions (Wenger, 2012). The following educators talk about how their careers have unfolded in continuous and discontinuous ways. In the sections that follow, we talk about these multiple roles, how authentic educators find their roles, and how the multiplicity and authenticity affect the way they see themselves. We also discuss changing roles as educators move from position to position.

Multiple Roles. Frequently early childhood educators are with children all day to comfort and guide, facilitate and explain, and converse and instruct. In this way, the job has built-in discontinuities. At times empathetic, at times directive, the early educator is often both simultaneously.

Paradoxically, the job's multiple and sometimes contradictory dimensions can combine to create a continuous relationship with children. A Spanish teacher spoke to us about the discontinuity she experienced when she saw the children only "in little pieces" and did not have the continuity and overview one gains from the multiple roles of daily life with children.

Culture and Style

My continuity comes from being able to be in the classroom in multiple aspects, sharing multiple roles. I started off as a part-time Spanish teacher for children pre-K through 6th grade. I met with most classes only once a week. It was very discontinuous. I would only see them in little pieces. Each classroom has its own culture, and I have my style, too. Each time I came into a classroom, I had to re-establish trust and management for myself and the kids. It wasn't until my role at the school expanded into becoming the director of aftercare as well as a floater aide in the lower grades that I really felt I was able to connect with the kids and therefore teach them on a better level. I was able to hang out with kids in a less academic manner. That helped me to know each student better and be able to teach to their individual needs and interests. It has totally changed the way I teach them. Kids whom I found difficult in the classroom shine in aftercare, and knowing them there helps me know what to do when I'm teaching Spanish.

Here is yet another example of the connection between continuity, trust, and relationships. In this case, continuous contact with the children resulted in relationships based not only on the teacher's knowing the children but also on their knowing and trusting her and her style.

Role Authenticity. In the next story, the same teacher describes her discomfort when her director asked her to pretend that she did not speak English. She further supports her contention that when children interact with their teacher's genuine identity, the teaching and learning relationship flourishes.

The Gig Would Be Up

I was working as a Spanish teacher during the school year. The director asked me not to speak any English to the children. She worried that if I spoke English to them, "the gig would be up," and the children would only speak English to me. That summer I worked for the same program with the same children, and this time I was allowed to use English as well as Spanish. I formed close relationships with the children, and when I was their Spanish teacher again in the fall and spoke only Spanish, they communicated with me in a whole new way. Now they saw me as a real person. They knew me in a different way and could read me and my facial expressions in addition to having more Spanish and being able to understand my language. They were more motivated to try to speak Spanish to me because they wanted to communicate with me. They knew me now.

When this teacher spoke to the children in English and Spanish, she was true to herself and her bilingual nature. Pretending to be unable to speak English was inauthentic. When she could be honest about who she was, she relaxed and developed real relationships with the children. From her telling, the children responded differently to her when she was genuine and thus trustworthy—when her teaching persona was continuous with who she is.

Mobility and Progressions. A seasoned educator told us about the diverse roles she played throughout her career and how, in retrospect, each job prepared her for the responsible position from which she plans to retire soon. Others told us about jobs they left and about the discomfort they experienced starting a new position.

Some early childhood career moves are natural next steps. Without disparaging her earlier experiences, a caregiver of infants told us that her personal trajectory demonstrates her continuous professional growth and positive changes as an early educator.

From Family Child Care to Center-Based Care

I have about 27 years of experience working with children. For 24 years I was a family child care provider. I worked with children from ages 3 months to 4 years. One of the first children from my family day care home just started college. I'm so excited. It's good for me to see them grow. I know the children. I'm with them so many years.

Then, when my children were grown, I decided to work outside of my home. It was my own goal. Now, I have my CDA [Child Development Associate Credential], and I'm working here at this infant-toddler program. I'm glad to be here. I have a lot of experience.

While her move to center-based care fulfills a professional goal for her, she values her work as a family child care provider, the relationships she developed in that capacity, and the skills she gained through that work. Moving to center-based care with a new credential enables her to continue steadily on her professional path. Using skills she has always had, for example, her native language, and mastering new information about child development, she has confidence and feels comfortable in her new role. While the change provides new challenges, she now has colleagues and supervisors with whom to reflect on her work with children and families.

Educators experience discontinuity within their career trajectories as well. An executive director who began as a teacher in the program told us about experiencing both continuity and discontinuity.

Alone at the Top

There's the obvious continuity of remaining in this place for most of my career. Kids don't change, but politicians and bureaucracy do.

I've been working in this neighborhood for over 25 years, and I'll run into families on the street or children who I taught at 4 years old, now all grown up. Anyone who remains in the same place long enough gets to see the outcomes of the lives they've had an impact on. I get to have the knowledge and experience and remember all that from so long ago, but now it's at a different level. But it gives you that grounding, which reminds me of why I entered this field.

As a teacher, I had more direct contact with children. Now as an administrator, I'm rarely in the classroom. That's where I should be [pointing to the office]. There's discontinuity, because relationships with staff change over time. As an administrator, you're looking at things from a different perspective. Even though there's a sameness, there's a different relationship. You're alone at the top. I sometimes feel isolated. It can be attributed to either growth or stagnation.

This director describes continuity. The neighborhood remains the same, as does the knowledge of and experience in early childhood education that hopefully grounds an administrator's work. The director has grown into a new position, now working with former peers in a new way. And this creates discontinuity. The director muses that not everyone grows in the same way. Perhaps discontinuity arises now because the director, teachers, family workers, and education coordinator no longer share the perspectives that they used to share. A director holds power over the others at the center, and that may disrupt relationships as well.

This director followed a steady path from teacher to executive director. Not all early childhood educators want to or feel pressure to move into new roles or to take on administrative responsibilities. This director raises the question of what it means to grow as a professional. Some people see professional growth as moving along a continuum of increasing supervisory responsibility. Other educators choose to remain teachers or staff developers, and growth for them may involve knowing children, families, and colleagues more deeply and having fulfilling relationships with them.

When teachers, directors, and others who work with children move from position to position, that change can disrupt the comfort of the known, and the early childhood educator may experience some kind of identity upheaval.

Switching Jobs

Switching jobs after 17 years was hard. For all my complaints at the infant center, I was there. It takes a long time to feel settled in a place, to feel a part of it. Even after 4 years at my new job, I sometimes think I don't really belong here the way I did there—however, that took an awfully long time, too, to feel settled there.

This director's story illustrates how familiarity with a job engenders a sense of continuity and comfort, but one with which she was not fully satisfied. When she sought a new position to escape the situations about which she had complained, she experienced the discontinuity of a challenging new job. The unsettling job changes this director described may in part be attributed to productive discontinuity.

Nonetheless, discontinuity and the lack of knowledge of or inability to control a new setting can generate a feeling of powerlessness. As we spoke to early educators who told other stories related to their identities, power and powerlessness emerged as a theme.

POWER AND POWERLESSNESS

Issues of power exist in early childhood classrooms (Dahlberg, Moss, & Pence, 1999). As Overton (2009) found, when external forces exert power over teachers and teachers lose their ability to make decisions about their own classrooms, teachers are disempowered. For example, a school district mandates a didactic kindergarten literacy curriculum; then the educators who believe in the effectiveness of a balanced literacy program feel constrained. They can no longer teach reading in ways that are consistent with their identities as teachers. From the stories we heard, early childhood educators wield power and endure powerlessness. As the following sections show, both seem to lead to discontinuity.

Powerful Teachers

Early childhood educators take care of other people's children—an enormous responsibility. Parents vest power in teachers and count on them to know about children, care for them, and guide and teach them. Parents may regard teachers as powerful, particularly if their own teachers were unapproachable authority figures. Some teachers have more education or professional training than the families with whom they work, and, though not well paid, their education and income place them in a different socioeconomic class from that of the parents. In other situations, early educators work with families who exercise privilege and treat educated teachers like babysitters. In either case, and in many others, such factors can lead to the discontinuity of a power differential.

We heard from an educator who became a home visitor after working in an infant room. Her director recruited her because she is bilingual. She noted that as a classroom teacher she knew the children better but had less time for parents. Now, as a home visitor, her primary relationship is with the entire family. She forges close relationships with them and delights in her ability to help them. Her problem-solving abilities afford her a sense of power in her new position.

Little Hero

Most of the parents I see do not speak English and have no papers. I asked one parent why her 3-year-old child didn't talk. The child, mother, and father lived in one small room. The mother was afraid that if the child made any noise, the landlord would kick them out, and they would have no place to live. I realized that since the child is a U.S. citizen they qualify for housing support and a better place to live. I helped them to get that. Once I support a family like that, I get closer to them. I can help solve problems and find a way out. That makes my relationships with families closer as a home visitor than they were when I was a classroom teacher.

I feel like a little hero. A parent was looking for an apartment in a cheaper area. I found something for her. With another family, I searched for the nearest library and we went together. We found out they have English classes and homework help. It was like this mother had won the lottery. And I feel like I accomplished something faster than I do in the classroom.

From this story we hear the joy that the teacher feels from helping families to reach community resources to find housing and English language classes. She described her new role as a problem solver, a "little hero" who can accomplish good for the families she serves.

Helping others is congruent with images of early childhood educators as nurturing and kind. As this teacher described, solving problems for families is rewarding and enables her to build relationships with the families, who are grateful to her. She offered them resources they both wanted and needed. Yet her situation is a tricky one. The dynamic can create a power imbalance between the family and the professional. This discontinuity can be unhealthy for the professional who identifies as a savior and the family who feels dependent upon her.

Teachers have skills and knowledge in many areas, including child development, curriculum decisionmaking, and methods to support diverse needs and interests. This home visitor also had fluent English, which the families did not have, and knowledge of resources for families. This expertise contributes to an educator's teaching identity. Yet when teachers share their expert knowledge, the message to families can be "I'm in charge here." This approach can place families in a passive role, the recipient of the teacher's decisions rather than a partner with the educator (Turnbull, Turnbull, Erwin, Soodak, & Shogren, 2010). Awareness of the power differential can help teachers reflect on the decisions they make and the impact on their ever-developing identities.

As you see from the "Little Hero" story, teachers can join families as partners or distance themselves as experts. In the next story, the teachers face this dilemma.

I Asked Her Not To

We've encouraged a mom of a particularly shy child to take her out so that she is around other people. Although the mom likes to stay home after working all week, she's started doing it. I rode the train with the two of them the other day. Her mom used to cover up the stroller when they were on the train. I asked her not to, so people could see the child and interact with her. I've been talking to the mom about taking her daughter out even when she cries, and now the child says "Bye, see you later" to her mom in the morning.

The teachers in this story thought about the child, determined that she would benefit from becoming more outgoing, and turned to her mother to meet their goals for the child. The mom, who did not want to go out herself after working all week, complied with the teachers' request for what they believed was good for her child. We do not know if they elicited the mother's reasons for, or feelings about, keeping her child away from other people. From this telling, the teachers use the power vested in their professional identities to instruct the mother. This story is a reminder of the importance of listening carefully and eliciting explanations from families to share power with them.

Powerless Educators

While the teacher's role can be powerful, in some situations teachers have little or no power. They may work for institutions whose policies take power away from the teacher. They may work for an authoritarian supervisor. Their sense of powerlessness leads to feelings of discontinuity with children and families or with a program at which they work.

Educators with No Say. A large institution or a program serving a specific population may have regulations that teachers do not contribute to framing but to which they must adhere. A teacher at a treatment center for mothers told us about her experience.

The Treatment Community

I work in a residential child care house. Our families stay with us for 9–15 months at most. While the children are in our care, we show the mothers "how" to parent or show new ideas to them and try the ideas together. When the children are with us, we have a community to support each other, to do what we can. We only have our children for that short time, though, while their mothers are in treatment. We have a transition period for children before the children and mothers leave the facility. When mothers leave treatment, the professionals can't contact them. So we have continuity *and* discontinuity in our homes. Once they leave our "community" we are no longer able to maintain a relationship with the family. We can't go up to them in the street. It's hard not to contact them, but it's just not appropriate. If they see us in the community, children will run to the teachers, although we cannot initiate contact with them. With regard to having continuity, we do, but we don't.

In this story the teachers teach the parents, with the same power as in the previous two stories. They also build relationships, as the previous two teachers may, too. That continuity with children and families becomes an aspect of their teaching identities. However, in this story, paradoxically, the continuity is shattered for the teachers, families, and children just as the parents and children's lives are about to improve. The relationships that teachers and parents worked to forge and that supported children cannot continue as the family moves from the therapeutic setting into the larger community.

In this story, the teachers understood why they could not continue relationships with the children or families, although they found the restriction difficult and upsetting. The next story provides an example of misunderstanding and perhaps retribution that led to a teacher's sense of powerlessness and discontinuity.

It Was Weird

Early Head Start is really big on continuity. You only have four kids and you move up with your group. You team teach with someone else that has four children. I started with the 1-year-olds and stayed with them until they were almost 3. Now, this is what was weird. I became pregnant, and my director pulled me from the group of children I had worked with for 2 years and put me with new younger kids. This happened the day I told her I was pregnant. She said it was for continuity of care and because I couldn't be with the kids until they transitioned out of the program, I had to start with a new group that was not attached to me. It was so emotional for me, and I started crying. How was that any different than if I left a few months later? How would having a new teacher for a few months be better continuity of care for my group of kids?

The next day I walked to the playground, and my four kids were looking at me and their eyes said, "Why are you with these other kids?" You should have seen the look on their faces. We had no good-bye and the parents were not even informed of the change. A parent came to me and asked what happened, and I sent them to the director for an explanation—I didn't know what to think or say!

Did the director move this teacher because she was angry at her for getting pregnant and leaving? Or was the director misguided about continuity of care and how it builds relationships? In either case, the teacher felt punished and powerless. The continuity she had built with children was disrupted, as was her identity as their caring teacher.

Teachers are not the only ones wondering how much power they have. The coordinator of a quality rating and improvement system (QRIS) told us how she felt about a program she was assisting to meet state standards. She became suspicious that the program operated differently during her scheduled visits than it did on a daily basis.

It Burns Me Still

I started to "drop in" but as soon as someone saw my car, things inside the center would change. I parked down the road to walk in without notice, but that didn't work either. I couldn't pull the center out of QRIS, because of what I never saw. It burns me still. I had no control. You get to a certain professional level yourself, and you really care about quality and what is best for children and families. I could not make this situation better and couldn't decide whether to keep trying or get the heck out of there.

Despite her "professional level" and ostensible power over programs, she was unable to control this situation. You can hear her frustration and anger as she told how a center director thwarted her work.

The resulting powerlessness has a double impact on her identity as an early childhood leader. First of all, she cannot implement her vision of quality care, and that vision is essential to her identity as a leader (Simon, 2015). Second, her experience with this center leaves her uncertain about what to do, putting her off balance. Confidence and assurance that what she is doing is right seem to be essential components of her identity as a leader.

The Low Status of the Field. External views of early care and education, early educators' internal perceptions of their status, and the reality of poor compensation affect teachers' sense of themselves. For example, teachers are conscious of the power associated with working with older age groups. A director told us that this issue was most salient for those working or about to work with the very youngest children.

Knocked Back Down

The big problem is the undervaluing of infant teachers. Only one teacher is proud of being an infant teacher. They feel like infant teachers are at the bottom of the barrel. They're ashamed of being infant teachers. One teacher didn't want members of her church to visit and see she works with infants. Another, whose mother is a pre-K teacher, thinks becoming an infant teacher after her children finish the 2s group is "being knocked back down." Some people who work in the infant or toddler rooms see working in pre-K as a step up.

When these teachers undervalue work with infants, their attitudes mirror the predicament of the early childhood field as a whole: the older the children, the more power and prestige for the teacher. Ochshorn

(2015, p. 60) points to the "cognitive dissonance" inherent in a professional early childhood identity that members of the education community disparage. How other professionals and the society at large view early childhood educators and their work with the youngest children necessarily affects how infant caregivers view themselves.

Early childhood educators' status is more than a matter of perception. Most of them receive low pay for hard work that requires professional training and judgment. A staff development specialist told us the following story.

Poverty Wages

Because the teachers are paid so little, they are living in poverty just as the parents are. The families experience domestic violence, and so do the teachers. The children see family members arrested, and their teachers may have that experience as well. Children's family members are unemployed or underemployed. Child care workers experience ongoing underemployment themselves as they make poverty wages and have high expenses relative to their income, paying for their own health insurance, for example.

The staff development specialist told us that these teachers' program attempts to break the poverty cycle by providing quality early learning experiences for young children. Unfortunately, this story calls us to consider how programs that are designed to help children move out of poverty can leave the early childhood educators who work in them in continuing impoverished circumstances. The reality of low pay and low status necessarily affects teachers' identities.

PHILOSOPHICAL CONTINUITIES AND DISCONTINUITIES

An additional issue related to power arises as early childhood educators negotiate their personal and professional selves and one takes precedence over the other. An early childhood educator's teaching identity rests on adopting philosophical positions (Alsup, 2006). As early childhood educators develop their teaching identities, they integrate their personal qualities with the culture of early childhood education to greater and lesser degrees.

Academic training and workplace colleagues as well as the professional literature and conference sessions supply a presumably commonly held doctrine (Sachs, 2010, p. 153). Since early childhood ideology is closely related to child-rearing practices, educators can experience discontinuity between their personal, professional, and teaching identities.

Adopting a professional early childhood education identity may go fairly smoothly for someone whose family and cultural background is more or less in synchrony with developmentally appropriate practice. For anyone else, outsider status can make taking on the stereotypical teacher identity more difficult (Alsup, 2006). Yet no singular or universal function can define teachers outside the contexts of their teaching and their personal histories (Ryan & Grieshaber, 2005). Various discourses define the early childhood educator differently, and one can find many ways to be a good early childhood teacher.

Discontinuity Between Self-Perception and the "Ideal"

The teacher in the next story struggles with the expectation that she look the part of an early childhood teacher.

The Way I Look

As an early childhood educator, I don't look like a typical educator. So I have been asked in my career to change the way I look and behave to model how females should be. This has been a discontinuity for me. In my own way I have represented alternative ways of being in early childhood. I've actually been asked to wear earrings, pretty shirts, don't wear jeans. I put continuity in terms of maintaining status quo, continuing the gender binary or hierarchy of male–female.

For this teacher, outward appearance becomes a philosophical issue. She maintains that gender bias and heteronormativity are at the root of conventional images of a good early childhood teacher. This teacher's presentation of self creates contradictions or discontinuity for colleagues and parents. As Grieshaber (2008) suggests, she challenges the dominant discourse on what it means to be an early childhood educator and, in doing so, interrupts the assumed consensus. However, everyone's teaching identity goes well beneath a surface impression.

According to Warren (2014), "Teachers acting in acceptable and normal ways in their professional settings are viewed positively by others and gain credibility, status and power" (p. 187). One's professional identity is inextricably linked to the dominant discourses within the field from which it draws its power. When professional and personal perspectives are continuous, issues of power are less evident. In fact, the individual may take the power for granted. Discontinuity raises the question of whether anyone's values, beliefs, and ways of being should be privileged over others.

Using Teacher Knowledge When Parenting

Teachers who are also parents may face the challenge of integrating their teaching persona with their personal persona as a parent. Teaching differs from parenting, and one's relationship with other people's children is necessarily neither as close nor as fraught with emotions as with one's own child. Here is what one teacher told us about applying knowledge from her professional preparation and ongoing work with children to her relationship with her own children.

Stuck and Knowing It

When I started college I had my first child. I was thinking about majoring in business but decided to take an infant course to learn how to be a good parent. I took the course and really latched on to it. I learned so much—brain development, talking during diapering, and pointing out the infant's red pants rather than using a flash card with the color red on it . . . how to talk to children so they really listen and the concept of natural consequences for misbehavior.

So as a parent I used all the strategies I learned about in the teacher education program. When my child drew with markers on the living room wall the markers were taken away for a while. There was no other real punishment. Boy, it flipped on me! One day when Frannie was in 1st grade she did something, I can't remember what, and when I told her what would happen to her because of her misbehavior she threw my words back in my face—"Why is that my punishment? It does not fit what I did wrong." As she grew older and would get into trouble and I would come up with a consequence she would tell me, "No, I really want to talk about this." I didn't want to become an authoritarian parent, but I was stuck and knew it.

Here is a teacher with a continuous and consistent set of beliefs that seem to apply to her family life. Nevertheless, while she can be consistent in her professional practice, her parenting comes from a deep place with much personal history. As the applicability of educational theory breaks down in personal practice, her multiple roles create a perhaps necessary discontinuity.

Juggling Philosophies

Alsup (2006) raises the question of how much one has to adopt a new persona when embarking upon a career in teaching. Novice early childhood educators learn early childhood ideology in teacher education programs and in children's classrooms with their supervising teachers. The developmentally appropriate practice that students learn in teacher education programs and that programs across the country strive to implement is based on middle-class Western values (Lubeck, 1998) that differ from what some teachers practice at home. For many, this discontinuity requires them to reconcile their personal and professional identities. One teacher told us about her identity shifts as she moved between home as a parent and school as a teacher developing a new identity with children.

Hats

It is tricky as a parent and a teacher. Who I am as a parent and who I am as a teacher is dramatically different. I do one thing for my students, then I go home and do something completely different for my children. My language, my demeanor, my patience, my attitude—all are different when I am with my own children, and I feel okay with that. If they [my own children] were on the verge of getting in trouble, I would count (quickly) and if I made it to five, they would get a timeout or, depending on the severity of the offense, they might have gotten grounded. These are the things you have to wrestle with on a daily basis. I step in one door as a teacher and put on my "teacher" hat with the accompanying attitude of, "All right everyone, I'm here, let's play, let's have fun today and see where the day is going to take us." Then, I arrive home, and the "mom" hat goes on, which communicates, "It's time to get down to business, and this is the way it is."

This teacher describes her identity shifts or changes in hats as she moves between home and school. She embraces the philosophy and value system of the center where she works and interacts with children there accordingly. Her home identity is more authoritarian; while at school she puts on a hat that has her looking from a child's perspective. Despite the disparity between these two identities, she seems comfortable moving between the two. Unlike the parent in the previous story, she does not attempt to merge them.

Philosophy and Upbringing

The situation may be different for teachers whose cultural values conflict with those embedded in developmentally appropriate practice and who teach in the community in which they were raised and now live. A director of a community-based therapeutic program spoke to us about this mismatch.

I Can't Do This

The valuing of learning from play—our teachers have never played themselves. We've discussed the different uses of toys and equipment. They say, "You can't take messy stuff home. You can't play with it. You play with dough only when making biscuits. If grandma comes in and sees you, you'll get beaten for playing with dough. Why you wasting food?" It's really difficult to ask some of our teachers to let children play in certain ways. Some younger and some older teachers say, "No, I can't do this." It depends on how they were raised and what they value, no matter what their education is. People are always falling back to cultural norms.

This director recognizes that "the claim that quality standards follow in some simple and direct and value-free way from scientific discovery is spurious" (Tobin, 2005, p. 426). In her role as director, she raises questions with the staff about play, observing that allowing children to play is foreign to people who have not experienced it themselves. She goes on to say, "Where play becomes so valuable is in the extension of the play; that's where the learning is. That's the hardest thing to work with staff on." Together, she and the teachers do an identity dance involving the personal identities at the core of who teachers are and the behaviors that she, as the director, believes will support children's growth and learning.

Another story illustrates how this negotiation of identities can work. A teacher reported how her insider knowledge as a member of the cultural community enabled her to listen respectfully and understand children's meanings as they played. As a result, she learned about them as she played with them.

Red Cups and White Cups

When children trust us, we can see what happens at home. Children code-switch behaviors. I played with two girls who were 2½ and 3 and were getting ready for a party. We have clear cups and other cups that are white on the inside and red on the outside. In the community, those are liquor cups, because they hide what's inside and have markers inside to show how much liquor you've poured. One child told me I was the child. She asked, "Do you want milk or muscatel? The other girl got a red cup for muscatel. They told me, "You have to have milk, and you have to get out of our face, because you are the baby." This is what children will do when they really trust you.

This teacher negotiated her identity as a teacher with her community member self. She embraced play in a way she could not have done without knowing the children and their context.

CONCLUDING THOUGHTS

Professional identity construction, then, is a social enterprise best seen not as a set of polarities or binaries but as a process. We act in the early childhood worlds we populate with children, families, and colleagues, and those actions establish our evolving teaching identities. The flexible and dynamic process of creating and re-creating our professional selves is fraught with discontinuities that both stretch and stymie us. At the same time, continuity and coherence stemming from gratifying work with children and families and the communities we inhabit with them afford us comfort. As Himley (1991, p. 49–50, emphasis in original) writes:

> We find ourselves *in* life, *in* motion, acting in the world, thoroughly implicated *in* a peopled landscape, witnessing and gathering up our lives as we live them. Within the wide expanse of possibility that opens up between the ongoingness of life and abrupt deviations of course, we can for different purposes come down either on the side of continuity and connections or that of radical change and discontinuity. That is when, experiencing or recollecting our lives, we can emphasize threads running through time and connecting events, or we can highlight disjunction and jarring moments of dramatic change. It seems to me both emphases are true and each is partial.

CHAPTER 6

Conclusion

If Everything's Perfect, Nobody Grows

The Program We Really Wanted

I was the program director for a private nonprofit center that had two sites: an infant-toddler program with two rooms and 21 children and a large preschool site for 160 children, 2 to 5 years old. Despite our efforts to have children from the infant site visit the other site and our invitations to parents of toddlers to come for tours of the preschool, no one felt good about children's huge transition between the two sites. Parents of children making the transition to the bigger site reported to their children's former teachers that the preschool and its yard were too big, with too many children; that no one knew the children; and that it was not as cozy and homelike as the infant-toddler program.

When we were in danger of losing our rent subsidy for the infant-toddler site, the leadership team, which consisted of the executive director, the administrative director, the development director, and myself, realized we would have to combine the two programs to make a go of it financially. The infant-toddler program with its high ratio of staff to children couldn't sustain itself without support from the preschool. As we talked about construction of a consolidated program, we saw that it was a good time to change our structure and develop the program we really wanted.

As this story unfolded, the program director told us how a crisis led to changes that the program leadership hoped would increase continuity for children and families as they moved from the infant program to the preschool. Changes introduce discontinuities, too, both productive and disruptive ones. Any transition between systems or settings within a system creates an opportunity for continuity and discontinuity.

In the remaining pages, you will read more about this program and the complexities of the changes it underwent. We use this extended story to highlight the implications of continuity and discontinuity for early childhood practice. As you read the program director's story and consider the questions it raises, we hope that you will see applications to your own

practice and ways in which your thinking about continuity and discontinuity will enrich the work you do.

THEMES OF CONTINUITY AND DISCONTINUITY

As you have seen in the preceding chapters, issues of continuity and discontinuity thread through every aspect of early childhood education.
Thinking about continuity and discontinuity raises questions about how
to structure programs that are responsive to children and families and
about the relationships that develop between educators, children, and
families in those programs. Considering continuity and discontinuity leads
educators to query both the large systems that connect children's and
families' experiences and their individual experiences as ever-developing
professionals. These investigations range from the broadest to the most
immediate.

One of the primary themes of this book has been the macro and the
micro and the ways in which they work together. The macro of policies and
structures frame what occurs at the micro, or local, level where individual
children, teachers, and families connect one experience to the next. Macro-
level decisions and mandates can set the stage for the relationships and
practices that make sense in context, but they cannot make meaningful
relationships and thoughtful practices happen. Confounding or conflicting
policies superimposed on the existing ecology of a program can interfere
with practice at the local level. And although policymakers can mandate
structures in the hopes of continuity, real continuity takes time and emerges from the nature of the interactions between people, across cultural communities, and among structural systems. Teachers' and directors' actions
matter. They bear the responsibility of knowing the children and families
and making relationships with them work. They can also influence the systems that policymakers shape, just as those systems affect them.

For example, the structure of continuity of care can foster close relationships, but those relationships depend upon the individuals involved.
The program aims to create a warm community and develop a relationship with every child and family. The system of continuity of care is a
means to achieve it that depends upon the constant effort the program
professionals make. If the system, in this case continuity of care, becomes
the goal without attention to the original purpose of the structure, a program can risk poor quality and will do little to improve children's and
families' lives (Klein, 2012). In contrast, if the center staff creates continuous experiences for children and families that fit the local context and
include discontinuity as a healthy factor, the teachers and administrators
create structures and systems for themselves.

A second theme counters the assumption that continuity is always desirable. Instead we argue against a disregard for the possibilities that discontinuity can offer. Returning to the example of continuity of care, on the one hand, children, families, and staff experience the warmth of their relationships. On the other, those relationships enable children to separate and move on. The separation may be difficult and may cause sadness, and then the ability to negotiate discontinuity is a life skill. Furthermore, children's often ambivalent eagerness for the transition and subsequent discontinuity of moving on is a sign of growth. Continuity and discontinuity are both part of a positive picture.

A third theme, based on Urie Bronfenbrenner's ecological systems theory and Lev Vygotsky's sociocultural theory, recognizes the multiple contexts in which children and families develop and the interactions between these contexts or systems. Social relationships that are continuous and discontinuous are integral to children's learning and development, to their families, and to their teachers' ongoing professional growth.

Educational settings for children are complex living, evolving systems. They meet criteria for complexity in that they are "self-organizing, self-maintaining, and tend to be nested within (arising from and giving rise to) other systems" (Davis & Sumara, 2008, p. 36). The interrelatedness of continuity and discontinuity in early childhood settings is one aspect of this complexity.

Since continuity and discontinuity intertwine and coexist and are based on the individuals involved, their interactions, and their lived contexts, neither continuity nor discontinuity provides a single answer. Instead, programs and individuals can seek the comfort of continuity *and* the stimulation of discontinuity, as you will see as the story continues.

Building Continuity, Building Community

As the story that opened this chapter continued, the program director described how she assembled resources and then included the staff in multiple discussions from the beginning:

> My first step was to figure out the cost of bringing the infant-toddler program over to the preschool site. We had a development team and determined how much private and public money we had to raise. We went to our board of directors and presented the plan, the cost, and their role. Over a year before the actual consolidation, with board approval and the money we needed to do the construction and implementation, we began talking about the new program structure at every staff meeting. Everyone on staff understood the financial considerations. We talked a lot about the programs and

how we could keep the culture of the infant-toddler program—the cocoonlike space that nurtured children and families alike.

Two-year-olds were originally in the preschool, but they behaved like 2s and not like preschoolers. Threes teachers wished the 2s teachers would prepare the children for preschool. Twos teachers felt pressure. With our new structure, 2s became the oldest children in the newly structured infant-toddler center. They moved from there as a group to a 3–4s classroom, and our discussions helped everyone understand that preparing children for the 3s class is not the 2s teachers' job.

The program's leadership team wanted everyone on board with the big change. They provided the context for philosophical alignment, comfort, and trust that leads staff members to feel connected to their work and, in this case, to the big change ahead. Although financial considerations are not usually within the purview of teachers and assistant teachers, knowledge and understanding of budgetary concerns enable everyone to share the vision, its possibilities, and its constraints. Everyone became part of the system that would be their new program.

In talking about how to keep the culture of the infant-toddler program, the program examined what that culture was, clarified roles, such as those of the 2s teachers, and identified the culture's valuable qualities. For example, the infant teachers did not want to sacrifice the cocoonlike feeling that they and families valued for the children. The program embraced continuity of those qualities rather than continuity for the sake of continuity.

In making a change with its inevitable upheavals, the program took account of multiple perspectives. Everyone, teachers of each age group and staff at every level of responsibility, had a voice. To understand one another's points of view as well to share their visions of the joint project, everyone needed a common language. To understand each other, they also needed support for their growing relationships with one another.

Everyone understood the benefits of continuity and of staying with children for more than 1 year, but there were many concerns about how it would work and anxieties about the changes. When we started planning for the move, both centers had been working with a team of mental health consultants. These consultants were instrumental in providing additional time and space to discuss the move and the new structure. All of the staff from both sites had gone through Center on the Social and Emotional Foundations for Early Learning (CSEFEL) training. Teams went to the training together because we found it didn't work for the head teacher to go to training and try to bring back what she learned. Through the CSEFEL training, we shifted our focus to the building of deep, supportive relationships with the children, families, and each other. We found a common language for talking about children's behaviors and learned to adjust environments to them. When confronted with challenging behavior, we put our effort into defining the function of the behavior and figuring out how the child could get what they needed without acting out inappropriately. In addition, all of the infant-toddler caregivers received Program for Infant/Toddler Care (PITC) training, the basis of which is responsive and individualized caregiving. With these supports in place I felt that we were at a point as an agency that we successfully could withstand the upheaval that would naturally come from such a huge structural change.

Attending training sessions together built relationships within each team and provided shared vocabulary for talking about their work with children. While the change they anticipated was structural, the program used the opportunity to build continuity for children through shared commitment to knowing children well and to learning about the contexts in which the children live. Everyone learned about understanding rather than condemning children's behavior and finding ways to work with children whose behavior was not acceptable to the staff. The new program practiced continuity of care and, most important, emphasizing continuity with who children are.

Policy and Structure

As the staff prepared for their big change and created a new system, they became part of larger systems as well. They used these systems to enhance their program's strengths.

The foundation of CSEFEL's pyramid for Supporting Social Emotional Competence in Infants and Young Children is "an effective workforce" and "systems and policies [that] promote and sustain the use of evidence-based practices." In addition to our many discussions about creating more continuity, we recognized that continuity of care is not a cure-all.

We knew we would experience many discontinuities and would need administrative support. People worried that even with continuity of care, teams never stay the same. A parent reported her child crying every night after a teacher left. Yet although we had a 40% turnover rate before we implemented the structural change, 3 years later turnover was only at 5%. I attribute that to the policies we implemented. We raised salaries to match the highest in our area; we made substitute teachers part of our program to cover classrooms with known adults so that teachers always got consultation sessions, and we did out-of-classroom team-building events. We added administrative staff and social service personnel, so that those jobs lessened some of the teachers' loads. These supports made the change possible. The teachers and the program as a whole were at a good place to take on the extra burden of the transition.

The program used external systems, such as CSEFEL, to solve problems together. The program director tells of systems that support the program's goals of helping teachers do their jobs well and developing cohesive teams. Rather than superimposing an alien system with irrelevant or even conflicting requirements on their program, the system grew to meet the needs of the educational community and the families and children it served.

The program director continued:

For the first 2–3 months of our planning, the infant-toddler staff talked about the move to their mental health consultants at weekly meetings. I was waiting to hear someone else suggest that teachers should stay with the same children for the children's first 3 years. As soon as that happened, I pulled out all the research I'd done on what people have done at other centers. We had always done primary caregiving, even in the preschool, and had been creating small groups; continuity of care was the third piece that this structure enabled us to have. I originally suggested birth to 5-year-olds in one room, but that was too much for people to hear.

The proposed changes and the idea of staying with children for more than 1 year had impact on the preschool teachers, so they quickly became part of the conversation. We decided that the preschool teachers would remain in the same room for 2 years with the same children. The preschool classrooms became either 3–4s rooms or 4–5s rooms. Each year, the teachers and children remained together, and teachers swapped materials and equipment to give the children what they needed. They supported teachers who hadn't worked with an age group before. On their own initiative they did workshops for other teachers. The way teams work with other teams has been a huge benefit for the center. Classrooms had been islands unto themselves. Now they started talking about children's transitions in February. Staff members have formed friendships across teams. That didn't happen in the preschool much before. There's cooperation and understanding. After 2 years, those teachers knew their children really well.

Here is a clear example of a group's implementing new policies that they developed from the ground up. The micro (the staff of this specific program) determined the macro (the continuity of care structure). The program's dedication to plenty of discussion prior to the change drew in the preschool teachers, who had previously been at a separate site and had not been in conversation to this degree with the infant-toddler teachers. The system that is the new program developed organically and in a way that made sense.

In the course of the big change and its new developments, the leadership team built in opportunities for reflection. Respect for the teachers, their ideas, and what they were ready to hear fed the process of their transforming professional identities. Everyone grew as the program changed.

Continuity, Discontinuity, and Diversity

All programs implement policies and practices that affect the children, teachers, and families. Since people are diverse, some of these policies and practices will fit their worldviews, while other policies and practices will not make sense to them. Diversity enriches any endeavor with multiple perspectives, but it also introduces discontinuity.

Trusting, committed, and reliable relationships between teachers and children, between staff and families, and between staff members can transform that discontinuity from a problem into an asset. Each of these relationships becomes stronger through communication. They flourish when all parties listen carefully to perspectives that differ from their own and acknowledge everyone's strengths. Then teachers can learn from the children, the families, and each other, taking an inquisitive stance and interrupting their own expectations (Delpit, 1988). Understanding culture, language, and structural power relationships can deepen early childhood educators' awareness and assist them as they navigate relationships. In the case of the adults, shared information enables them to work together to understand the child and each other.

The program in the unfolding story had a commitment to everyone understanding one another, to including everyone in the vision, and to making policies and practices comprehensible to everyone. The program director told us how diversity increased discontinuity in a helpful way:

Our centers serve a diverse group of families and children who pay differing amounts depending upon their income eligibility. For some children, especially those whose home environments have less stability, behavior during transitions is an issue. Discontinuity is an issue for families, too. After finally forming an attachment to a teacher, it's hard for the child and family to move to a totally different environment.

Like our families, our staff is diverse; many of them do not have advanced degrees, which are not required in our state; and many have a first language other than English. All of the information about the move and policy changes needed to be accessible. As we worked together to prepare for the structural change, I disseminated information from PITC, Zero to Three, and the Department of Education, breaking down material into little bites without leaving out anything. To make it easier to talk to parents—families from the infant-toddler site were in a panic about losing their space and moving to the preschool site that was so big—I wrote up talking points. Before this, a survey revealed that parents believed staff and administration were out of touch with each other. Teachers who couldn't explain policies would tell parents who asked for explanations, "I don't know. They just told us to do it." The talking points provided language, and teachers were able to articulate ideas they embraced but didn't have the words for.

Teachers have a range of perspectives because of their backgrounds as children and their experiences as adults. Even if their philosophies are in sync with the program's vision, inaccessible language makes it impossible for them to explain policies, practices, and the reasons for them. In fact, inaccessible language keeps families from understanding the program philosophy as well. Transparent language can build bridges while at the same time honoring discontinuities.

Continuity, Discontinuity, and Change

To increase continuity, early childhood educators navigate the transitions and new relationships that occur in a big change and, in fact, every day as children and families move from home to school. Teachers increase continuity through accommodations they make as they learn from children and families, but they also deal directly with discontinuity. Ending her story of the "Program We Really Wanted," the program director illustrated how her program viewed continuity and discontinuity as reciprocal, not contradictory, concepts:

We dedicated monthly parent meetings to the move. Ordinarily I didn't attend those meetings, since the site directors did, but I went to all of the ones about the move. As a program, after 6 months of discussion, we had pretty unanimous agreement. Not one person quit over our structural change.

We asked for feedback every step of the way. For example, each group had a name. Children stayed in the same group with the same group name from the time they entered until they were 3. Parents told us that when their children transitioned to preschool they needed to be in a group with a new name. That was important to the children who looked forward to being big kids upstairs. We learned from them that the transition to preschool was a valuable step for the children. A lot of things were like that. Learning comes out of disruption. We kept in mind that if everything's perfect, nobody grows. The challenge is, in times of discontinuity, to have supports in place that lead to positive outcomes, to success.

Although the staff aimed to smooth out bumps in children's experience and create continuity as much as possible, they were open to parents' reports that children wanted acknowledgment of their growth and change. The children liked their preschool classrooms' new names. They were proud of the discontinuity that was emblematic of their growth.

APPLYING THEMES OF CONTINUITY AND
DISCONTINUITY TO YOUR PRACTICE

The new program's teachers, administrators, and families built continuity by reinforcing their togetherness. As much as possible, they created relevant policies and structures as a team, communicating constantly with one another. They recognized that continuity and discontinuity are inextricable from one another. Embracing both enabled their community to capitalize on its diversity and make change that worked. Together the program adults took the time and found the resources to make sense of the program they created together.

Any teacher's work is full of discontinuities and contradictions. On a daily basis, early childhood educators juggle nurturing children with scaffolding their self-regulation through natural consequences and integrate both roles into their evolving teaching identities. Disappointed in systems that are supposed to improve early childhood education, many teachers are left powerless to implement what they consider good for the children and families with whom they work.

Even without the catalyst of a big change, early childhood educators must make sense of their work with children and families in a larger, evolving sociopolitical context. While the program this chapter describes managed to raise salaries, for many educators, poor wages and low status add to their sense of discontinuity.

Philosophy and ideology ground everyone's work with children (Alsup, 2006). The teachers, administrators, and parents in this story seemed to come to agreements. However, educators cannot take such continuity for granted. When someone's belief system or identity differs from a program's norms, everyone has an opportunity for growth if they examine their biases and how they make meaning. This is an ongoing process with no pat answers.

A program's curriculum and interactions may not resonate with a teacher's philosophy. Perhaps the program tries to save money with too few adults in the room or uses videos or workbooks instead of allowing children to explore and express themselves. Perhaps a teacher is uncomfortable at a center that unquestioningly follows aspects of developmentally appropriate practice despite cultural dissonance with teachers or families' personal belief systems.

Clearly, the job is fraught with continuities and discontinuities to make sense of and navigate. Here are some final thoughts and questions to consider as you do that work:

> *Relationships with children and families require close attention and conscious effort.* While structures and policies are apparent, the elements of what make relationships work are elusive and hard to pinpoint. What enriches and deepens your relationships with children, families, and colleagues?
>
> *Policies and practices to support continuity make sense when they are based on what teachers know about the children and the families in their communities.* Early learning standards, developmentally appropriate practice, and many systems built to create continuity establish developmental expectations that generalize about children. How do you learn about the children, families, and community with whom you work? How do you apply what you know about them to create continuity for children and families and negotiate discontinuity with them? How do you apply what you know about yourself and your beliefs about teaching and learning?
>
> *Early childhood practice at both the micro and macro levels demands sustained focus on who children are and awareness of the different ways in which each of them learns.* Children deserve attention. Systems that hope to prepare young children for their movement into elementary school have their eye on progress but can overlook the children as they are in the present. How will you advocate for systems that keep their eyes on the child?

Knowing children well can help teachers plan curriculum and can inform families about their children. Yet some programs collect data in ways that do not demonstrate what children know or can do or that are not useful to teachers and families. What data is worth gathering on young children? How can you use data to convince funders that your work is worthwhile? What data are most useful to you as you work with children and families? How can you advocate for that type of assessment or program data?

Early childhood education grows out of different philosophies, resulting in different approaches. This historical lack of consensus and cohesion is a discontinuity that can undermine or strengthen work at the micro and macro levels. How do different approaches to children arise in your work? In what ways does your awareness of differing viewpoints about children and families make you better at your work?

Early childhood policies and practices at national, regional, and program levels influence continuity and discontinuity for children and families. Yet continuity is ultimately contingent on the interactions between individuals and their environment. This means that individuals—children, their families, and their teachers—have agency. They are the ones in relationship with one another in the sociocultural contexts of the past and present.

Relationships are at the core of early childhood education. Developing and maintaining relationships is messy work that has no set prescription. Systems and structures that focus on children and can change and grow to fit children in diverse communities can support connections within programs. When agencies and professionals know and continue to learn about children and families, they can help children expand on past experiences and contexts as they continue to grow and learn.

References

Ackerman, D. J. (2008). Continuity of care, professional community, and the policy context: Potential benefits for infant and toddler teachers' professional development. *Early Education and Development, 19*(5), 753–772.

Adams, R., & Persinger, J. (2013). Research-based practice: School support and same-sex parents. *NASP Communiqué,* 42(2). Retrieved from www.nasponline .org/publications/cq/42/2/school-support.aspx

Aguillard, A. E., Pierce, S. H., Benedict, J. H., & Burts, D. C. (2005). Barriers to the implementation of continuity-of-care practices in child care centers. *Early Childhood Research Quarterly, 20,* 329–344.

Aina, O. E., & Cameron, P. A. (2011). Why does gender matter? Counteracting stereotypes with young children. *Dimensions of Early Childhood, 39*(3), 11–19.

Alsup, J. (2006). *Teacher identity discourses: Negotiating personal and professional spaces.* Mahwah, NJ: Lawrence Erlbaum Associates.

American Academy of Pediatrics, American Public Health Association, National Resource Center for Health and Safety in Child Care and Early Education. (2014). *Caring for infants and toddlers in childcare and early education. Applicable standards from: Caring for our children: National health and safety performance standards; Guidelines for early care and education programs* (3rd ed.). Elk Grove Village, IL: American Academy of Pediatrics; Washington DC: American Public Health Association. Retrieved from nrckids.org

Baker, A. C., & Manfredi/Petitt, L. A. (2004). *Relationships, the heart of quality care: Creating community among adults in early care settings.* Washington, DC: National Association for the Education of Young Children.

Baker, A. L., Kessler-Sklar, S., Piotrkowski, C. S., & Parker, F. L. (1999). Kindergarten and first-grade teachers' reported knowledge of parents' involvement in their children's education. *Elementary School Journal, 99*(4), 367–380.

Barnett, W. S. (2011). Four reasons the United States should offer every child a preschool education. In E. Zigler, W. Gilliam, & W. S. Barnett (Eds.), *The pre-K debates: Current controversies and issues* (pp. 34–39). Baltimore, MD: Brookes.

Barrera, I., & Corso, R. (2003). *Skilled dialog.* Baltimore, MD: Brookes.

Baumrind, D. (1991). The influence of parenting style on adolescent competence and substance use. *The Journal of Early Adolescence, 11*(1), 56–95. doi: 10.1177/0272431691111004

Bretherton, I., & Mulholland, K. A. (2008). Internal working models in attachment relationships: A construct revisited. In J. Cassidy, & P. R. Shaver (Eds.), *Handbook of attachment, second edition: Theory, research, and clinical applications* (pp. 89–111). New York, NY: Guildford Press.

Bronfenbrenner, U. (1979). *The ecology of human development: Experiments by nature and design.* Cambridge, MA: Harvard University Press.

Bronfenbrenner, U. (1986). Ecology of the family as a context for human development: Research perspectives. *Developmental Psychology, 22*(6), 723–742.

Bruner, C. (2012). A systems approach to young children's healthy development and readiness for school. In S. L. Kagan & K. Kauerz (Eds.), *Early childhood systems: Transforming early learning* (pp. 35–40). New York, NY: Teachers College Press.

Cabral, M. (2012). Curriculum models and identity: Three stories of early childhood teachers. *Literacy Information and Computer Education Journal, 3*(2), 544–553.

Cagliari, P. (2012). Continuity in learning: The Reggio Emilia approach and lifelong education. *Innovations in Early Education: The International Reggio Emilia Exchange, 19*(2), 1–5.

Caplan, J. G. (2000). Building strong family-school partnerships to support high student achievement. *The Informed Educator Series.* Arlington, VA: Educational Research Service.

Casper, V., & Theilheimer, R. (2010). *Early childhood education: Learning together.* New York, NY: McGraw-Hill.

Cassidy, J. (2008). The nature of the child's ties. In J. Cassidy & P. R. Shaver (Eds.), *Handbook of attachment, second edition: Theory, research, and clinical applications* (pp. 3–22). New York, NY: Guildford Press.

Center for Law and Social Policy. (2011, January). *Building comprehensive state systems for vulnerable babies: A resource for state leaders.* (Issue brief). Washington DC: Center for Law and Social Policy. Retrieved from www.clasp.org/resources -and-publications/files/system_components.pdf

Cheatham, G. A., & Jimenez-Silva, M. (2012). Partnering with Latino families during kindergarten transition: Lessons learned from a parent-teacher conference. *Childhood Education, 88*(3), 187–193.

Child Care Aware of America. (2015). *Child care in America: 2015 state fact sheets.* Retrieved from cca.worksmartsuite.com/GetThumbnail.aspx?assetid=675

Dahlberg, G., Moss, P., & Pence, A. (1999). *Beyond quality in early childhood education and care: Postmodern perspectives.* London, UK: Falmer Press.

Davis, B., & Sumara, D. (2008). Complexity as a theory of education. *Transnational Curriculum Inquiry, 5*(2). Retrieved from nitinat.library.ubc.ca/ojs/index.php /tci

Delpit, L. (1988). The silenced dialogue: Power and pedagogy in educating other people's children. *Harvard Educational Review, 58*(3), 280–298.

Dewey, J. (1938/1997). *Experience and education.* New York: Touchstone.

Dockett, S., & Perry, B. (2007). *Transitions to school: Perceptions, expectations, experiences.* Sydney, Australia: UNSW Press.

Dombro, A., Jablon, J., & Stetson, C. (2011). *Powerful interactions.* Washington, DC: National Association for the Education of Young Children.

Fabian, H., & Dunlop, A. (Eds.). (2002). *Transitions in the early years: Debating continuity and progression for young children in early education.* New York, NY: RoutledgeFalmer.

Fogel, A. (2009). *Infancy: Infant, family, and society* (5th ed.). Stanford, CT: Wadsworth.

Fonthal, G. (2004). *Alignment of state assessments and higher education expectations: Definition and utilization of an alignment index.* Retrieved from intedco.org /documents/pdf/GF_AlignmUS.pdf

Galinsky, E. (2010). *Mind in the making.* New York, NY: HarperCollins.

Gauvain, M. (2001). *The social context of cognitive development.* New York, NY: Guilford Press.

Geiser, K. E., Horowitz, I. M., & Gerstein, A. (2013). *Improving the quality and continuity of practice across early childhood education and elementary community settings.* Stanford University, John W. Gardner Center. gardnercenter.stanford.edu /resources/publications/GardnerCenter_RB_ECELinkages_2013.pdf

Gesell, A. (1943). *Child development: An introduction to the study of human growth.* New York, NY: Harper & Row.

Ghaye, A., & Pascal, C. (1988). Four-year-old children in reception classrooms: Participant perceptions and practice. *Educational Studies, 14*(2), 187–208.

Goffin, S. G. (2013). *Early childhood education for a new era: Leading for our profession.* New York, NY: Teachers College Press.

Goldstein, A., Hamm, K., & Schumacher, R. (n.d.). *Supporting growth and development of babies in child care: What does the research say?* Washington, DC: Zero to Three Policy Center & Center for Law and Social Policy. Retrieved from main .zerotothree.org/site/DocServer/ChildCareResearchBrief.pdf?docID=3542

Göncü, A., Abel, B., & Boshans, M. (2010). The role of attachment and play in young children's learning and development. In K. Littleton, C. Wood, & J. Kleine Staarman (Eds.), *Handbook of psychology in education.* Bingley, WA, UK: Emerald Group.

González, N., Moll, L., & Amanti, C. (2005). *Funds of knowledge: Theorizing practices in households, communities, and classrooms.* Mahwah, NJ: Erlbaum.

Gonzalez-Mena, J. (2005). *Diversity in early care and education: Honoring differences* (4th ed.). New York, NY: McGraw Hill.

Gonzalez-Mena, J., & Eyer, D. W. (2012). Infants, toddlers, and caregivers: A curriculum of respectful, responsive, and relationship-based care and education (9th ed.). New York, NY: McGraw-Hill.

Gottlieb, A. (2004). *The Afterlife is where we come from: The culture of infancy in West Africa.* Chicago, IL: University of Chicago Press.

Grieshaber, S. (2008). Interrupting stereotypes: Teaching and the education of young children. *Early Education and Development, 19*(3), 385–395.

Hart, B., & Risley, T. R. (1995). *Meaningful differences in the everyday experience of young American children*. Baltimore, MD: Brookes.

Himley, M. (1991). *Shared territory: Understanding children's writing as works*. New York, NY: Oxford University Press.

Hung, H. (2008). Teacher learning: Reflective practice as a site of engagement for professional identity construction. *US-China Education Review, 5*(5), 39–49.

Institute of Medicine & National Research Council. (2015). *Transforming the workforce for children birth through age 8: A unifying foundation*. Washington, DC: National Academies Press.

Kagan, S. L. (1991, September). The strategic importance of linkages and the transition between early childhood programs and early elementary schools. *1st National Policy Forum: Sticking together: Strengthening linkages and the transition between early childhood education and early elementary school* (pp. 7–10). Washington, DC: US Department of Education. files.eric.ed.gov/fulltext/ED351152.pdf

Kagan, S. L., & Kauerz, K. (2012) *Early childhood systems: Transforming early learning*. New York, NY: Teachers College Press.

Kagan, S. L. & Tarrant, K. (Eds.). (2010). *Transitions for young children: Creating connections across early childhood systems*. Baltimore, MD: Brookes.

Katz, L. (2013). General issues in teacher education. In M. Ben-Pertz, S. Kleeman, R. Reichenberg, & S. Shimoni (Eds.), *Embracing the social and the creative: New scenarios for teacher education* (pp. 3–20). Lanham, MD: Rowman & Littlefield.

Keats, E. J. (1976). *The snowy day*. London, UK: Puffin Books.

Keyser, J. (2006). *From parent to partners: Building a family-centered early childhood program*. St. Paul, MN: Redleaf Press.

Klein, L. (2012). Early childhood systems: An important means to an essential ends. In S. L. Kagan & K. Kauerz (Eds.), *Early childhood systems: Transforming early learning* (pp. 25–29). New York, NY: Teachers College Press.

Kosciw, J. G., Greytak, E. W., Diaz, E. M., & Bartkiewicz, M. J. (2008). *Involved, invisible, ignored: The experiences of lesbian, gay, bisexual, and transgender parents and their children in our nation's K–12 schools*. Gay, Lesbian and Straight Education Network. Retrieved from www.glsen.org/binary-data/GLSEN_ATTACHMENTS/file/000/001/1104-1.pdf

Kreider, H. (2002). Getting parents "ready" for kindergarten: The role of early childhood education. *Family Involvement Network of Educators (FINE) Newsletter*. Retrieved from www.hfrp.org/publications-resources/browse-our-publications/getting-parents-ready-for-kindergarten-the-role-of-early-childhood-education

Lally, J. R. & Signer, S. M. (n.d.). *Introduction to continuity*. WestEd, the Program for Infant Toddler Caregivers. Retrieved from www.pitc.org/cs/pitclib/download/pitc_res/360/Introduction%20to%20Continuity.pdf?x-r=pcfile_d

Leinaweaver, J. (2014). Informal kinship-based fostering around the world: Anthropological findings. *Child Development Perspectives, 8*(3), 131–136.

Letts, W., & Simpson, T. (2003, May 1–4). *Plunge into the deep: Knowledge construction through "othering" oneself.* Paper presented at the Our Children the Future 3 conference, Adelaide Convention Centre, Adelaide, Australia.

Lightfoot, S. L. (1978). *Worlds apart: Relationships between families and schools.* New York, NY: Basic Books.

Lombardi, J. (1992). *Beyond transition: Ensuring continuity in early childhood services.* (ERIC Digest No. ED345867 1992-00-00)

Lubeck, S. (1998). Is developmentally appropriate practice for everyone? *Childhood Education, 74*(5), 283–292.

Mapp, K. L. (2003). Having their say: Parents describe why and how they are engaged in their children's learning. *School Community Journal, 13*(1), 35–64.

Maxwell, B., & Racine. E. (2012). Does the neuroscience research on early stress justify responsive childcare? Examining interwoven epistemological and ethical challenges. *Neuroethics, 5*(2), 159–172.

Mayfield, M. (2003). Continuity among early childhood programs: Issues and strategies from an international view. *Teaching Strategies, 79*(4), 239–241.

National Association for the Education of Young Children. (2009). *Developmentally appropriate practice.* Washington DC: National Association for the Education of Young Children.

National Early Childhood Accountability Task Force. (2007). *Taking stock: Assessing and improving early childhood learning and program quality* (Report of The National Early Childhood Accountability Task Force). Retrieved from www.pewtrusts.org/~/media/legacy/uploadedfiles/wwwpewtrustsorg/reports/pre-k_education/taskforcereport1pdf.pdf

National Infant and Toddler Child Care Initiative. (2010). *Relationships: The heart of development and learning.* Washington, DC.: Office of Child Care Administration for Children and Families, U.S. Department of Health and Human Services, & Zero to Three. www.zerotothree.org/public-policy/state-community-policy/nitcci/multidisciplinary-consultant-module-1.pdf

Nelson, C. A., Fox, N. A., & Zeanah, C. H. (2014, December 2). Forgotten children: What Romania can tell us about institutional care. *Foreign Affairs.* www.foreignaffairs.com/articles/142409/charles-a-nelson-nathan-a-fox-and-charles-h-zeanah/forgotten-children

Neuman, S. B., & Roskos, K. A. (1994). Of scribbles, schemas, and storybooks: Using literacy albums to document young children's literacy growth. *Young Children, 49*, 78–85.

Nieto, S., & Bode, P. (2008). *Affirming diversity: The sociopolitical context of multicultural education* (6th ed.). New York, NY: Allyn & Bacon.

Noddings, N. (1991). Caring and continuity in education. *Scandinavian Journal of Educational Research, 35*(1), 3–12.

Ochshorn, S. (2015). *Squandering America's future: Why ECE policy matters for equality, our economy, and our children.* New York, NY: Teachers College Press.

Overton, J. (2009). Early childhood teachers in contexts of power: Empowerment and a voice. *Australian Journal of Early Childhood, 34*(2), 1–10.

Peters, D. L., & Kontos, S. (1987). Continuity and discontinuity of experience: An intervention perspective. In D. L. Peters & S. Kontos (Eds.), *Continuity and discontinuity of experience in child care* (pp. 1–16). Norwood, NJ: Ablex.

Ponder, K. (2012). A state vision for an early childhood system: Meaningful governance. In S. L. Kagan & K. Kauerz (Eds.), *Early childhood systems: Transforming early learning* (pp. 41–46). New York, NY: Teachers College Press.

Raikes, H. H., & Edwards, C. P. (2009). *Extending the dance in infant and toddler caregiving: Enhancing attachment and relationships.* Baltimore, MD: Brookes.

Regional Educational Laboratories' Early Childhood Collaboration Network. (1995). *Continuity in early childhood: A framework for home, school, and community linkages.* Washington, DC: Administration on Children, Youth and Families, U.S. Department of Health and Human Services, & the Office of Educational Research and Improvement, U.S. Department of Education. www.sedl.org /prep/hsclinkages.pdf

Rimm-Kaufman, S.E., & Pianta, R.C. (2000). An ecological perspective on the transition to kindergarten: A theoretical framework to guide empirical research. *Journal of Applied Developmental Psychology, 21,* 491–511.

Rochat, P. (2001). *The infant's world.* Cambridge, MA: Harvard University Press.

Rogoff, B. (1994). Developing understanding of the idea of communities of learners. *Mind, Culture, and Activity, 1*(4), 209–229.

Rogoff, B. (2003). *The cultural nature of human development.* New York, NY: Oxford Press.

Rouse, L. (2012). Family-centered practice: Empowerment, self-efficacy, and challenges for practitioners in early childhood education and care. *Contemporary Issues in Early Childhood, 13*(1), 17–26.

Ryan, S., & Grieshaber, S. (2005). Shifting from developmental to postmodern practices in early childhood teacher education. *Journal of Teacher Education, 56*(1), 34–45.

Sachs, J. (2010). Teacher professional identity: Competing discourses, competing outcomes. *Education Policy, 16*(2), 149–161.

Schaack, D., Tarrant, K., Boller, K., & Tout, K. (2012). Quality rating and improvement systems: Frameworks for early care and education systems change. In S. L. Kagan & K. Kauerz (Eds.), *Early childhood systems: Transforming early learning* (pp. 71–86). New York, NY: Teachers College Press.

Scott, K. H. (2012). Vision vs. reality: The real challenge of large systems development. In S. L. Kagan & K. Kauerz (Eds.), *Early childhood systems: Transforming early learning* (pp. 18–24). New York, NY: Teachers College Press.

Scully, P. A., Seefeldt, C., & Barbour, N. H. (2003). *Developmental continuity across preschool and primary grades: Implications for teachers* (2nd ed.). Wheaton, MD: Association for Childhood Education International.

Sendak, M. (1963). *Where the wild things are.* New York, NY: Harper & Row.

Simon, F. (2015). Look up and out to lead: 20/20 vision for effective leadership. *Young Children, 70*(2), 18–24.

Stern, D. (1985). *The interpersonal world of the infant.* New York, NY: Basic Books.

Sullivan, M. (2012). *Continuity and curriculum: The impact of high quality education in the PK–3 years.* Master's thesis, University of Minnesota. Retrieved from conservancy.umn.edu/bitstream/handle/11299/123596/Sullivan_Continuity%20and%20Curriculum%20The%20Impact%20of%20High%20Quality%20Education%20in%20the%20PK%20years.pdf?sequence=1

Thelen, E. (1995). Motor development: A new synthesis. *American Psychologist, 50*(2), 79–95.

Tobin, J. (2005). Quality in early childhood education: An anthropologist's perspective. *Early Education and Development, 16*(4), 421–434.

Tronick, E. (2007). *The neurobehavioral and social-emotional development of infants and children.* New York, NY: Norton.

Turnbull, A. A., Turnbull, H. R., Erwin, E. J., Soodak, L. C., & Shogren, K. A. (2010). *Families, professionals, and exceptionality: Positive outcomes through partnerships and trust* (6th ed.). Upper Saddle River, NJ: Pearson.

U.S. Department of Education. (2011). Race to the Top—early learning challenge application for initial funding (CFDA Number: 84.412). Retrieved from www2.ed.gov/programs/racetothetop-earlylearningchallenge/2011-412.doc

Valdez, G. (1996). *Con respeto: Bridging the distances between culturally diverse families and schools; An ethnographic portrait.* New York, NY: Teacher's College Press.

Vygotsky, L. S. (1978). Mind in society: Development of higher psychological processes. M. Cole, V. John-Steiner, S. Scribner, & E. Souberman (Eds.). Cambridge, MA: Harvard University Press.

Warren, A. (2014). "Relationships for me are the key for everything": Early childhood teachers' subjectivities as relational. *Contemporary Issues in Early Childhood, 15*(3), 185–194.

Wenger, E. (1998). *Communities of practice: Learning, meaning, and identity.* Cambridge: Cambridge University Press.

Wenger, E. (2012). Communities of practice and social learning systems: The career of a concept. Retrieved from wenger-trayner.com/wp-content/uploads/2012/01/09-10-27-CoPs-and-systems-v2.01.pdf

Wood, E., & Bennett, N. (1999). Progression and continuity in early childhood education: Tensions and contradictions. *International Journal of Early Years Education, 7*(1), 5–16.

Zeanah, C. H., Anders, T. F., Seifer, R., & Stern, D. N. (1989). Implications of research on infant development for psychodynamic theory and practice. *Journal of the American Academy of Child and Adolescent Psychiatry, 28*(5), 657–668.

Index